NITY COLLEGE

D0603879

the
Feminine
Face *of*
Buddhism

the Feminine Face of Buddhism

Gill Farrer-Halls

Quest Books
Theosophical Publishing House

Wheaton, Illinois ◆ Chennai (Madras), India

Copyright © 2002 Godsfield Press
Text copyright © 2002 Gill Farrer-Halls

First Quest Edition 2002
Copublished with Godsfield Press 2002

The Theosophical Publishing House
P.O. Box 270
Wheaton, Illinois 60189-0270

Designed for Godsfield Press by
The Bridgewater Book Company

Library of Congress Cataloging-in-Publication Data
Farrer-Halls, Gill.
The feminine face of Buddhism/Gill Farrer-Halls. — 1st Quest ed.
p.   cm.
Includes index.
ISBN 0-8356-0821-2
1. Women in Buddhism. 2. Women—Religious aspects—Buddhism.
3. Feminism—Religious aspects—Buddism. I. Title.
BQ4570. W6 F37 2002
294.3'082--dc21   2002066753

Printed and bound in China

1   2   3   4   5   6   7   8   9   10

The Theosophical Publishing House
is aided by the generous support of
THE KERN FOUNDATION,
a trust established by Herbert A. Kern
and dedicated to Theosophical education.

Bridgewater Books would like to thank the following
for permission to reproduce copyright material:
Amaravati Monastery: p.36. Martine Batchelor: pps: 31, 49, 83,
98, 99, 101, 125. Robert Beer: pps:1, 2, 8–9, 11, 15, 18, 21, 22,
46–47, 53, 54, 55, 56, 59, 60, 65, 68, 76, 77, 84, 86, 92–93, 94,
103, 104, 108–109, 111, 113, 121, 122, 124, 126–127, 128. Bill
Bettencourt: p.34. Bridgeman Art Library: p.114, Arthur M
Sackler Museum, Harvard University Art Museums, USA. Corbis:
pps: 3, 19, 26–27, 28, 44, 48, 62, 66, 70–71, 72, 74, 75, 78, 88,
95.Yahne le Toumelin: p.104. Millicent Harvey: p.82. Nomad
Pictures: pps: 51, 116, Brian Beresford; 90, Michael Marchant.
Sharda Rogell: p.42. Renate Seifarth: p.32. Tibet Images: pps: 5,
Fuchsia Dunlop; 12, Nick Dawson; 25, B. Luther. Wolfgang
Hurten: p.40.
Front cover: Corbis; back cover: Robert Beer.

CONTENTS

Introduction

Like the world's other great religions, including Christianity, Islam, Judaism, and Hinduism, Buddhism has historically been seen and heard through a predominantly male viewpoint. The philosophy and beliefs of Buddhism are not at fault for this lack of feminine perspective. Rather, the problem lies in the Asian cultures in which Buddhism originated and to which it spread in the first few centuries after the Buddha lived. Traditional Asian attitudes toward women are quite different from the modern Western view. As Buddhism has traveled West, these attitudes have caused concern, misunderstanding, and even hostility. *The Feminine Face of Buddhism* seeks to go beyond the male orientation in Buddhism to explore the female vision and experience of Buddhism, which has until recently lain in the shadows of history and culture.

We begin by looking at the lives of women during the time of the Buddha. We learn from them what it was like for women to practice the Buddha's path during his lifetime, and bear witness to their struggle to be acknowledged as being as capable as men of purely following his teachings. Then we hear from some of the most interesting women practicing Buddhism today. Their stories span various roles, nationalities, and individual spiritual paths. Each woman's story of her encounter with the Buddha's teachings is unique and contributes to an overall picture of how Buddhism is experienced by contemporary women.

We explore the role of women as Buddhist teachers and meet several outstanding examples. We also examine how the feminine is represented in Buddhist art and meet three Buddhist women artists. We are inspired by reading about Buddhist female deities, whose symbolic enlightened figures represent enlightened feminine qualities. In the final chapter, we look at the Buddhist quality of wisdom, traditionally considered to be feminine, together with its complementary quality of compassion, considered to be masculine. As we see, the feminine figure of the *dakini*, one of the principal icons of Tibetan Buddhism, reveals the inseparable nature of wisdom with the female principle.

However, there is no point in revealing the feminine face of Buddhism if the motivation is to suggest that the female perspective is superior to the

male. To do so would be to fall into an historical and cultural trap like the one that created the original inequality. Rather, as we discover, an essential purpose of practicing the Buddha's teachings on awakening is to move us beyond the duality of male and female, beyond the ego identification of being a woman or a man. For the dedicated Buddhist practitioner, obsession over gender issues is, at worst, a minor distraction and eventually becomes simply irrelevant.

My experience as a modern Western woman who is also a Buddhist has sometimes been challenging. But I have received nothing but kindness and compassion from my Tibetan teachers. Despite their cultural background, I doubt that they ever thought of me as inferior to their male students, and even if they did, this attitude was never shown and therefore never became a problem. The problems I have experienced have usually arisen from my own confused mind and my misunderstanding of the teachings. So I feel nothing but immense gratitude at having been fortunate enough to encounter the Buddha's teachings in my lifetime.

But my personal experience, and the positive experiences of other women, does not negate the fact that there have been problems for women in Buddhism. The inequality caused by traditional hierarchies needs to be addressed, and *The Feminine Face of Buddhism* does not shy away from these difficult issues. However, the book seeks mainly to honor Buddhism's feminine archetypes, celebrate women's contributions to Buddhism, and document the critical role women have played and are playing in the development of Buddhism through their lives, their work, their practice, their teaching, and their art. My intention is to bring a balance to traditional ways of presenting Buddhism, to allow us to see women's experiences and hear women's voices as different from but complementary and equal to those of men.

In the end, it is practicing what Buddha taught that is important. Whenever I become distracted by gender-based thinking and apparent discrimination against women, I try to remember the wise comment of Tara, the compassionate female bodhisattva: "Here no man, no woman." Just someone on the path to enlightenment.

This book has been possible for me to write only because of the great kindness of all my teachers, Tibetan and Western, women and men. I thank them all deeply. I hope this book brings the wisdom of the feminine face of Buddhism to everyone who reads it.

CHAPTER ONE
EARLY BUDDHIST WOMEN

Sukka you are light
Because of your bright mind.
The wise drink her words
As travelers drink rain
And never tire of their sweetness.
—SAMYUTTA NIKAYA

Early Buddhist Women

Women's stories have not been told. And without stories there is no articulation
of experience. Without stories a woman is lost when she comes to make important
decisions in her life. She does not learn to value her struggles, to celebrate her strengths,
to comprehend her pain. Without stories she is alienated from those deeper experiences
of self and world that have been called spiritual or religious.
—CAROL CHRIST, QUOTED IN TSULTRIM ALLIONE, *WOMEN OF WISDOM*

Most people know the story of the Buddha and how Buddhism developed. As with the origin stories of many religions, it is a story that features a man and is told from a male point of view: Prince Siddhartha was born around five hundred years before Christ into a ruling family of the Shakya clan, in north India. In his late twenties, he renounced the royal life of luxury to follow a religious path, and after six years of spiritual endeavor, attained enlightenment sitting under a peepul tree. The Buddha, as he had now become, spent the rest of his life teaching everyone who sought his wisdom and creating a monastic order for those who wished to follow him in the homeless life of a mendicant. After he died at eighty years old, his teachings spread throughout Asia and became known as Buddhism.

However, many women also figure in the historical origins of Buddhism. The Buddha was surrounded by women as well as men throughout his life, including family members such as his mother, wife, and aunt. Over the next centuries, many other women followed his teachings on their journeys to enlightenment. It is time to tell their stories, to balance male-only Buddhism with Buddhism's feminine face, to celebrate the spiritual endeavors and wisdom of the women who walked and still walk Buddha's path.

The Buddha's Mother

The first person intimately connected with the Buddha was, of course, a woman—his mother. Mahamaya was born into the Koliyan clan, most likely the daughter of a nobleman. She was married to Suddhodana, Siddhartha's father. Legend states that various prophetic dreams heralded her conception of the Buddha. Since he was no ordinary child, Siddhartha was also not conceived in the usual fashion, but descended from a Buddhist pure realm called Tushita in the form of a white elephant. Mahamaya had a long pregnancy that lasted ten months. When she was near to giving birth, she set out to travel to her family home as was the traditional custom.

Mahamaya and her entourage stopped to rest in the Lumbini Garden. While wandering and admiring the beautiful flowering trees, she felt her labor start and hung onto the branch of an asoka tree. According to legend, she gave birth painlessly to Siddhartha from her right side while standing,

Mahamaya, the mother of the Buddha, giving birth to him miraculously from her right side. | She is supporting herself during her labor with the branch of an asoka tree.

her death, she immediately entered a pure realm as a result of being the Buddha's mother. Over two centuries later, the Buddhist Emperor Ashoka honored the Buddha and his mother by erecting a pillar to mark the place of the birth, which still stands today.

The First Buddhist Nun

The baby prince was adopted by his aunt, Mahamaya's sister Mahapajapati, who was also married to Suddhodhana. She raised and cared for Siddhartha until he fled the palace on his spiritual quest. When he returned to his family home years later, he was no longer Prince Siddhartha; he was the Buddha, a religious leader whose reputation had preceded him. Mahapajapati was in her late fifties or early sixties by this time. She was esteemed because of her age and wisdom and because she was the wife of a nobleman. She welcomed the Buddha warmly, listened to his teachings, and immediately decided to take up the Buddhist path, which pleased the Buddha, who encouraged and supported her decision. At this time in India, it was unusual for a woman to have such privileged access to religious teachings, especially from a revered spiritual leader like the Buddha.

still supporting herself with the branch. The baby was born unstained, though water poured from the heavens over mother and child as a blessing. To the astonishment of all present, the newborn baby took seven steps in each of the four directions proclaiming that this was his last rebirth. However, this miraculous birth ended sadly for Mahamaya, who died seven days afterward. It is said that after

Many men from the extended family of the Shakya and Koliyan clans, who had heard the Buddha teach, became converts as well and went on to become ordained monks. Monks left everything behind and joined the Buddha in a homeless life, wandering from teaching to teaching, living in the forests, and begging each day for their food. Among the things monks left behind were their wives, mothers, and daughters, who were now without male support. In the Indian culture of the time, a woman gained her position in society through the men with whom she was affiliated; without male relatives, a woman lost status and respect. Mahapajapati was an exception due to her high standing and her close relationship with the Buddha. As a result, increasing numbers of women began to seek Mahapajapati's advice, support, and assistance after being abandoned by their men.

Many of these women soon came to relish their freedom from domestic drudgery and from their previous roles. No longer did they need to be wives, servants, dancing girls, or members of a harem—the chattels of men. Moreover, they were attracted to religious inquiry into the meaning of life and motivated to practice the Buddha's teach-

These modern Buddhist nuns, shown here studying a traditional Buddhist text, had much easier access to ordination than did Mahapajapati and the other early Buddhist nuns.

ings. These women formed a supportive network, willingly helping each other in practical matters and mutually encouraging each other's spiritual aspirations. Many of them had suffered in their lives; thus they had direct experience of and insight into the first of the Buddha's Four Noble Truths—the all-pervasive existence of suffering.

Mahapajapati realized she must take radical steps to help these women find an appropriate way to realize their spiritual aspirations. Since they were

already lay followers of the Buddha, these women were observing the rules laid down by the Buddha for such practitioners. These included following the eight moral precepts that govern daily behavior and conduct and listening to the Buddha's discourses held at the new, quarter, and full moon. The women also had various opportunities to ask questions and receive religious instruction from the Buddha and his senior monks. However, Mahapajapati recognized that these practices were an inferior version of the full spiritual lives led by the Buddha's monks. She resolved to ask the Buddha to ordain women into his official *sangha*, or community of followers, and to create an order of nuns.

Mahapajapati approached the Buddha respectfully with her request, but he refused her. Twice more Mahapajapati repeated her request, but each time she was refused, and she eventually left in tears. It seems clear that the Buddha was torn between the cultural conditioning of Hindu society, which stated that a woman's place was in the home and that her primary role was to bear children, and his understanding and conviction that women were as capable as men of spiritual practice aimed at enlightenment. The Jain religion that existed at this same time did have an order of nuns, though they were considered less spiritually able than their male counterparts. So while the instigation of Buddhist female ordination would have been radical and might have been thought to threaten social stability, it would not have been without precedent.

Mahapajapati was more determined than ever to become a nun. Shortly after his interview with Mahapajapati, the Buddha set out to walk to Vesali to teach in the Kutagara Hall in the Great Grove. Mahapajapati and some of her women shaved their heads, put on the saffron robes of monks, and then followed him on foot for one hundred and fifty miles, arriving exhausted and dusty. Disheveled and with swollen feet, Mahapajapati stood in tears outside the hall where the Buddha was teaching. Ananda, one of the Buddha's main disciples, saw her and asked her why she was crying. Mahapajapati explained to him that the Buddha had forbidden women to enter the homeless state of ordination.

Seeing her deep sincerity and the heartfelt desire of all the women to become nuns, Ananda resolved to take up their cause. He went himself to the Buddha and repeated Mahapajapati's request the traditional three times, but again, the Buddha refused. Then Ananda asked him if women were capable of realizing perfection and therefore of becoming enlightened. The Buddha answered that they could. Hearing this, Ananda repeated his original request.

This time, Ananda's plea was successful, and the Buddha agreed that the women could receive ordination. However, he laid down eight extra rules that nuns must follow in addition to those already in place for monks. The most contentious of these additional rules was that a nun, however learned and senior, must bow down respectfully before any monk, even an ignorant novice. In effect, this rule made nuns unconditionally inferior in status to monks. However, it seems clear that in adding these rules, the Buddha was making a compromise between the prevailing social norms and his inner conviction that women could attain *nirvana*, freedom from the cycle of uncontrolled death and rebirth. This compromise was the typical "middle way" of the Buddha, a path designed to minimize upset for all.

Thus the order of Buddhist nuns was created. When Mahapajapati was ordained, the Buddha gave her a subject of meditation through which she eventually attained enlightenment. She is reputed to have lived to be one hundred and twenty years old, remaining dedicated to the spiritual life and to nurturing the community of nuns until her death.

Traditional versus Revolutionary Roles

Mahamaya and Mahapajapati are often regarded as the Great Mothers of Buddhism, though their lives and experiences were quite different. We might say that Mahamaya represents the old order—behaving in the traditional way women were supposed to and earning her heavenly reward. Though highly regarded as the Buddha's mother, she is a passive, silent saint, who enters a pure realm through virtue of having given birth to the Buddha, rather than through striving for enlightenment on her own behalf.

Mahapajapati, on the other hand, represents the revolutionary. She rebels against traditional female behavior and creates a new order that helps liberate women from their domestic slavery and gives them freedom and control over their own spiritual lives. We might see her as a sister to Emily Pankhurst, who sacrificed herself to enfranchise women in twentieth-century England, and to all other women throughout history and all over the world who challenge the prevailing social order to help women gain equal opportunity with men.

In her courageous and radical way, Mahapajapati ensured that Buddhism, almost right from the start, allowed women the opportunity to dedicate their lives to the spiritual path by helping to introduce ordination for women. In one of her poems in the *Therigatha*, the collected poetry of these first Buddhist women and the earliest known collection of women's religious poetry, Mahapajapati honors and pays tribute to her elder sister Mahamaya, even though she herself had moved beyond these traditional female roles:

[Maha]maya gave birth to Gautama
[the Buddha]
For the sake of us all.
She has driven back the pain
Of the sick and the dying.

In a way, Mahapajapati was the true founding mother of Buddhism: She helped the Buddha establish the nuns' order and was the first ordained Buddhist nun and the first woman Buddhist teacher. She had her own disciples and inspired many of her contemporaries to follow her example in taking ordination and dedicating their lives to spiritual practice. Though women today might feel that becoming a nun lessens their freedom, given the social and cultural restrictions placed upon women in the time of the Buddha, Mahapajapati's nuns had much more freedom than they could have dared to imagine. Mahapajapati was among the first women to become enlightened in the Buddha's time. We can read her enlightenment verse in the *Therigatha*.

But I have seen the Blessed One;
This is my last body,
And I will not go
From birth to birth again.

The Buddha's Wife

Another woman in the Buddha's life was his wife Yasodhara, who was also his cousin. She was apparently very beautiful. The young Prince Siddhartha won her hand by being victorious in a series of contests with other suitors. The two were married when Siddhartha was only sixteen. The night that he fled the royal palace to pursue a spiritual life also happened to be the night that his son Rahula was born. When he returned as the Buddha, Yasodhara did not welcome the Buddha in the way Mahapajapati did. We might imagine that she felt abandoned by her husband, and upset. Nothing is recorded to tell us what happened to Yasodhara, though Rahula eventually became a monk and followed the Buddha.

The Buddha's apparently cruel behavior toward his wife might seem at odds with his teachings on love and compassion. However, he knew that the temporary gratifications of this life are not important compared to the lasting happiness of achieving nirvana. Thus his concern remained with those who sought to follow his teachings on the path to enlightenment. We can only surmise that Yasodhara was not interested in the Buddha's teachings. By contrast, the Buddha's half-sister, Sundari-Nanda (her name means "beautiful Nanda"), the daughter of Suddhodhana and Mahapajapati, was interested in the Buddha's message and received a powerful personal teaching from him. The Buddha declared that she had excellent meditative ability, foremost amongst the nuns. He taught Sundari-Nanda to meditate on the impermanence of her beautiful body, and using this meditation as her path, she attained enlightenment.

This ornate painting from the Ajanta caves in India depicts Yasodhara, the wife of the Buddha, with the Buddha.

The Story of Patacara

*One of the principles upon which feminist
historians have come to agree is ... to
concentrate upon how women acted rather
than how they were acted upon, and to
consider how women viewed events rather
than how women were viewed ... to view
women as active shapers of history and
interpreters of their own experience rather
than as passive objects or victims of history.*
—MIRANDA SHAW, *PASSIONATE ENLIGHTENMENT*

During the golden spiritual age when the Buddha
was alive, many members of his sangha were able
to attain enlightenment, including many nuns.
Lay life was considered inferior to the homeless
life of monastics, and we do not hear of laymen
or laywomen attaining enlightenment during this
period. However, it was recognized that not
everyone was ready to renounce worldly life, and
lay followers were encouraged to listen to the teachings and practice meditation and engage in other
spiritual activities as much as their life permitted.
Some lay people were inspired to renounce worldly
life and take ordination later, even when they were
quite old. For others, especially women, tragedy
and suffering brought them to the spiritual life, as
we can clearly see from the story of Patacara.

*Patacara was a strong and determined young
woman who defied her parents' wishes that she
marry their chosen suitor. She ran away instead
with a servant, who was already her lover. By so
doing, she renounced privilege and status and was
forced to live in a distant place in relative poverty.
In due course she became pregnant. Although she
attempted to reach her parents' house to have her
baby, her husband delayed her going, and she set
out on her own too late. While she was on the way,
her husband caught up with her and was with her
for the birth of their first child.*

*When Patacara was near to giving birth to her
second child, she again left for her family home
without her reluctant husband, taking her younger
child with her. Her husband caught up with her just
as a storm blew up. In his rush to cut wood to make
a shelter for her in the forest, he was bitten by a
snake and died. Patacara gave birth on her own and
used her body to protect her two children from the
storm. When the storm abated, she went to look for
her husband and was overcome with grief when she
discovered his body. There was nothing left for her
to do but make her way to her family and hope to
be taken in and looked after by them.*

*On the way Patacara needed to cross a river.
Since she could not carry both children at the same
time, she carried the newborn baby across the river
first, leaving him to rest on a pile of leaves while she
returned to get the elder child. However, when she
was in the middle of the river, she saw a hawk
snatch up the baby, and she shouted at the bird to
let the baby go. Hearing his mother cry out, the
elder child thought she was calling him and fell into
the river and drowned.*

*Filled with despair, Patacara stumbled on toward
her family's village. Near the village, she met a man
and asked him about her family. He told her that*

during the storm, the family's house had caved in, killing everyone inside. Patacara went crazy with grief. She wandered around in madness till her clothes fell off and the people drove her away with sticks. Still naked and crazy, she wandered into the Jeta Grove, where the Buddha was teaching. His disciples tried to keep her away, but the Buddha saw her and followed her. He placed himself in her path, and when they met, he said, "Sister, recover your presence of mind." Patacara came to her senses, realized she was naked, and gratefully covered herself with a cloak that someone threw to her. Then she asked the Buddha to help her. After hearing her tragic story, the Buddha told her that throughout

Bathing my feet
I watched the bath water
Spill down the slope.
I concentrated my mind
The way you train a good horse.

Then I took a lamp
And went into my cell,
Checked the bed and sat down on it.
I took a needle and pushed the wick down.

As the lamp went out
My mind was freed.

her many lives, she had shed more tears for the loss of loved ones than there was water in the oceans. He reminded her that at her death, even had they all been living, her family could only look on in helpless despair. Only the dharma, *his teachings, could help her to a better future life. Hearing this, Patacara asked the Buddha to ordain her. He did so and then took her to the nuns' community, which welcomed her in.*

Eventually, Patacara became one of the most revered female teachers, with thirty disciples. In the *Therigatha,* she is mentioned more than any other nun. Her enlightenment poem (see left) demonstrates that awakening can come in the midst of daily life and that seeking enlightenment is no different from engaging in a woman's everyday concerns.

There are many other stories of nuns who became enlightened. Some became great preachers, such as Dhammadina, who was regarded by the Buddha as the most gifted preacher among the nuns. Others, like Soma, retired to the forest and practiced solitary meditation sitting under a tree, a practice still followed today in the Thai Forest tradition of Theravada Buddhism. The women who chose to commit themselves to the Buddhist path came from all walks of life. Ordination can be seen as a great equalizer; every monk and nun is the same on the path to enlightenment. Thus, the nuns' community included former princesses, courtesans, prostitutes, mothers, wives, and old women. There was no discrimination. Just as Buddhist monasticism freed women from domestic servitude, it also freed them from caste and stereotypical social roles.

These lay women are making offerings to the Buddha, a traditional Buddhist practice. They may well decide to take ordination after meeting the Buddha.

The Relevance of Patacara's Story Today

These early Buddhist women deserve our gratitude and respect for setting an example for us today. The creation of the nun's order was the best way for these women to have the freedom to engage in meditation and spiritual practice. Though they had to put up with much opposition, and they coexisted somewhat uneasily with their monastic brothers and with society in general, their strength and spiritual commitment ensured that the nuns' community endured and flourished during the Buddha's lifetime. We can admire this fortitude and appreciate the high level of spiritual accomplishment of these nuns, which is apparent because so many of them attained enlightenment. Their example in turning away from a materialistic life and its temporary sensual gratifications is as relevant for us today as it was in a very different age and culture. These women also created the precedent of female spiritual authority in Buddhism, which modern Buddhist woman can emulate. When contemporary Buddhist women encounter difficulties and sexism on the spiritual path, remembering the struggles of these early Buddhist women can inspire them to stay the course.

We might think that these early Buddhist women have little in common with modern Western women who practice the Buddha's teachings. However, if we look at Patacara's story again, we might find aspects that are similar to our own life stories. Many of us rebel against our parents' wishes; we are attracted to unsuitable men and go off with them only to be let down by them in some fundamental way—even if this betrayal is less dramatic than their being bitten by a snake! We have our own issues around children and death and loss; some of us are unable to conceive, or we miscarry, or we need to have abortions, or we are not in a suitable relationship, or we are single and long to have children. These universal feminine problems can send us into a downward spiral, even bring on a nervous breakdown or a temporary madness like Patacara's. Perhaps our life crisis has nothing to do with procreation, but is brought on by an accident, or the loss of a job, or general unhappiness with our life. However, the experience of knowing suffering is the same for all women, and as Patacara demonstrates, extreme suffering can create a spiritual vacuum that brings with it a readiness for a radical change—what the ancient Greeks called *metanoia*.

If we are lucky, we find a spiritual teacher who understands the experience of suffering and can help lead us back to sanity and to understand that we need some form of spiritual practice to make sense of our experience. For some of us, this might be a Buddhist teacher. For others, it might be a therapist, who helps us get back on our feet so that we can later decide for ourselves that we need to follow a spiritual path. However, if we do not try to understand the causes of our suffering, and instead deny and repress our grief, we remain stuck, and our experiences do not move us forward in understanding the meaning of life. No amount of distractions or materialistic and sensual gratification can help us in the same way that self-inquiry and meditation can. The Buddha's teachings can still lead us toward liberation, in the same way that they helped Patacara over two thousand and five hundred years ago.

Present-day Buddhist nuns continue to faithfully follow the monastic code designed by the Buddha in much the same way the first Buddhist nuns did.

Women in Indian Tantric Buddhism

Tantra took centuries to come out of its closet … but it appears that originally, in the guise of fertility cults, it belonged to the pre-Aryan tribal worshipers of the Mother Goddess … One of Tantra's appeals was its catholic tolerance in initiating members of all castes and both sexes, a practice that militated against the priestly supremacy of the Brahmins.
—KEITH DOWMAN, *SKY DANCER*

After the Buddha died, inevitably there were changes for those who practiced his teachings. The Buddha had deliberately not collected his teachings in written form, nor did he create a centralized religion to preserve what he taught as a living tradition. However, after his death, his teachings did need to be codified, and so a council of five hundred monks established an oral tradition that remained in place for four hundred years until the Buddha's words began to be written down. Later councils debated changes to this tradition, after charges of degeneracy were laid against certain groups. Out of these schisms, eighteen different traditions arose from the original one, of which only the Theravada school remains today.

All of this upheaval in the establishment of early Buddhism occurred within a framework of Indian cultural and religious decline. Dry scholasticism dominated institutions of learning, and true spiritual practice was replaced by increasingly meaningless religious ritual. We hear little of Buddhist nuns during this period, but can assume the increasingly conservative mood led them to remain in the forest meditating, far away from a society that would not have tolerated the relative freedom they enjoyed during the Buddha's lifetime.

Meanwhile, from the beginning of the eighth century, the Arab powers were sending out armies to conquer fresh territory. Buddhist refugees from central Asia arrived in India with terrible tales of the destruction of Buddhist cultures, and it would be only a matter of time before these Islamic invaders reached India. Despite this looming threat—or perhaps because of it—Tantra evolved into a dominant spiritual practice, particularly in the Buddhist Pala Dynasty in Eastern India, which thrived until it, too, succumbed to the Islamic conquerors.

At the cutting edge of Indian Buddhist Tantra were the eighty-four *mahasiddhas*, men (and a handful of women) who rebelled against the crumbling conservative establishment. *Siddha* means "one who has attained enlightenment through the practice of Tantra," and *maha* means "great"; thus the mahasiddhas were "great Tantric masters of enlightenment." These practitioners often lived wild, itinerant, and free lives, boldly challenging the rigidity of caste and custom. Often known as divine madmen, they had developed magical powers, or *siddhis*, and were reputed to be able to fly in the sky and walk through solid objects. The mahasiddhas wandered mostly naked and covered in ashes, often spending time in charnel grounds, drinking from

human skulls, and inspiring whoever they encountered with their crazy wisdom. Four of the eighty-four traditional mahasiddhas were women, and though obviously in a minority, these women kept alive and celebrated women's role as dharma practitioners.

The Mad Princess Laksminkara

> *The Buddhas command*
> *that you must serve*
> *A delightful woman who*
> *will uphold you.*
> *A man who violates this*
> *is foolish and will*
> *not attain enlightenment.*
> —CANDAMAHAROSANA TANTRA

This contemporary painting of the Mad Princess Laksminkara after her enlightenment depicts her in the same dancing posture in which the deity Vajrayogini is traditionally represented.

The privileged young Princess Laksminkara lived a life of luxury, with all the benefits befitting her rank, in a beautiful palace in the Buddhist kingdom of Sambhola. She also received Buddhist teachings from the guru Kambala and other great teachers, and being spiritually ripe, she soon developed a deep understanding of many Buddhist Tantras. Her father had betrothed her at age seven to the son of Jalendra, a neighbor who ruled the nearby kingdom of Lankapuri, in order to strengthen the friendship between the two kingdoms. However, because Lankapuri was not a Buddhist land and because of Laksminkara's obvious spiritual ability, her father persuaded Jalendra to postpone the marriage ceremony until she was sixteen.

Inevitably the day dawned that Laksminkara must leave her family and her guru. She departed, accompanied by a large retinue and carrying many precious gifts for her new family. As the travelers neared their destination, a big hunting party galloped by, led by a young man with several deer carcasses and skins slung over his saddle. On learning that this young man was her husband-to-

be, Laksminkara felt deeply distressed at his most un-Buddhist behavior in hunting and killing the deer. When the princess arrived at King Jalendra's palace, her retinue was told to camp outside for a few days while court astrologers waited for an auspicious time for her to enter. This seemingly inhospitable behavior further troubled the princess.

The delay gave Laksminkara time to reflect upon her situation. All she really wanted was to practice the Tantric sadhana (ritual) that had been taught to her by her guru. As she waited, she saw other signs that Buddhism was not honored in her future husband's kingdom, which indicated that serious practice would be difficult. So the princess decided upon a radical solution. Opening the chests of treasures she had brought with her, she began to give away the contents to anyone who passed by. Finally, she gave her valuable jewelry to her servants and sent them home. Shortly afterward, she was invited into the palace. Immediately, she locked herself into a room, unbraided her hair, ripped her clothes, smeared herself with oil and ashes, and threw things at anyone who tried to approach her. Her husband-to-be quickly gave up the idea of marriage, as the young bride now seemed quite insane.

One night Laksminkara eluded her guards and escaped the palace. She made her way to the cremation grounds and remained there alone, practicing her sadhana and meditating, scavenging for scraps of food thrown to the dogs. Since her appearance and behavior indicated that she had gone mad, no one bothered her. Her extreme circumstances and deprivation created the opportunity for her to experience the visionary realm of mystical insight, and the Buddhas and bodhisattvas appeared to her and gave her teachings, including the female Buddha Vajrayogini. One day, an untouchable latrine cleaner from the palace encountered her and, recognizing her spiritual attainments, undertook to serve her faithfully. Once Laksminkara realized full enlightenment, she taught and initiated her servant, who swiftly attained enlightenment as well.

Some years later, when King Jalendra was out hunting in the forest, he lost his way. After searching for hours but failing to find his companions, he fell asleep under a tree. When he awoke, it was night. Seeing a light glowing in the distance, he made his way toward it. Stumbling upon a cave, he peeped inside and to his surprise saw Laksminkara, the woman to whom he would have wed his son but for her madness, seated on a throne, radiating golden light from her body and surrounded by adoring celestial goddesses. A deep faith arose in the king's heart, and he remained there till dawn, when he left to seek his companions. The faith that had spontaneously arisen within him at the sight of Laksminkara made the king return frequently to the cave and silently worship her.

One night Jalendra respectfully entered the cave, prostrated himself at Laksminkara's feet, and requested her to teach him. Surprised at the king's conversion, Laksminkara listened carefully to his repeated requests for teachings and his proclamations of faith until she was convinced he was genuine. She told him that she was not his guru, but *that he would find his guru among his servants—in the person of the lowly latrine cleaner, from whom he should seek instruction. Then she gave King Jalendra a teaching:*

All beings on the wheel of rebirth suffer,
For in samsara there is not one moment of bliss.
Even superior beings, men and gods, are tormented
While the lower realms are pain itself,
Where ravenous beasts constantly devour each other,
And some beings are ceaselessly tormented
by heat and cold.
O King! Seek the pure pleasure of release.
—QUOTED IN KEITH DOWMAN,
MASTERS OF ENCHANTMENT

Though Laksminkara's story seems to apply equally to both men and women who must suffer hardship to pursue the spiritual path, there is one aspect of Laksminkara's teachings that is very much rooted in women's experience. Among the Buddhas who came to Laksminkara in the charnel grounds to give her teachings was Vajrayogini, who appeared to the princess in a new form—naked, with long black hair and a yellow body, dancing and triumphantly waving aloft her own severed head. This central figure was surrounded by two

other dancing female figures, known as *dakinis*, which literally means "sky-goers." Three streams of blood poured from the neck of the central figure into the mouths of her two companions and the mouth of her own severed head.

This somewhat extreme image needs to be understood symbolically and as a meditation practice. Severing the head is symbolic of cutting attachment to the ego and thus eliminating dualistic thinking. The image of streams of life-giving blood flowing from a woman's body has biological associations and suggests that women can connect with the life energy within themselves and direct that energy toward spiritual realization. This practice is particularly relevant to women in that it does not deny the importance of the body on the spiritual path and reminds women that their own bodies can be the source of spiritual nourishment. Laksminkara transmitted the practice of Severed-Headed Vajrayogini to many female disciples and to her male disciple Virupa, who eventually took the practice to Nepal and Tibet.

Laksminkara's story also mirrors the life of the Buddha. Like him, she left a life of luxury and privilege to follow the spiritual path. Her life in the cremation grounds was austere in the extreme, as was the Buddha's period of ascetic spiritual practice. Also like the Buddha, after her enlightenment, she instructed disciples, gave teachings, and established certain practices.

Because of the extreme nature of Tantric practices, there are those who say that the rise of Tantra signaled the decline of Buddhism. But others, including His Holiness the Dalai Lama, explain that the Buddha himself taught the Tantras to a host of bodhisattvas and divine beings in another realm. Whichever position we hold, it is clear that the advent of Buddhist Tantra created a tradition that allowed women to practice without discrimination, while the original monastic form of Buddhism had by this time reduced nuns and women practitioners to a status substantially inferior to that of men.

Thus we can see a common thread running through these stories, those of the earliest women disciples of the Buddha and those of the later female mahasiddhas. Though all beings experience suffering, those who choose to follow the Buddha's path have the possibility of transcending suffering and achieving nirvana. However, men have traditionally been encouraged, supported, and revered in making the choice to pursue spiritual practice, while women

have had to fight against the prejudiced view that they are inferior to men, that they should stay in their place as faithful wives and child bearers, or that they are just not as worthy as men. Thus their experience of suffering often continued even after they had renounced the world and chosen the spiritual life, at least until they reached that stage on the path to enlightenment where all sufferings are seen as illusory.

Contemporary women practicing the dharma today may still have to contend with sexism, but they can take encouragement from the example of these early women practitioners, who are inspiring examples of spiritual courage, fortitude, and dedication.

These two Tibetan Buddhist nuns at Chiwong Gompa, Nepal, are an inspiration for meditators today.

CHAPTER TWO
CONTEMPORARY BUDDHIST WOMEN

If we want to have women
teachers in the West, we need some
practitioners. So it is up to you,
ladies, to practice and pass on the
fruits of your practice to others.

—ANI TENZIN PALMO

Buddhist Women Today

The lives of contemporary Buddhist women are quite different from those of the early Buddhist women profiled in the previous chapter. For one thing, the world has changed in many ways. Advances in technical and scientific knowledge have given us improved communications, longer life expectancy, and a wealth of material possessions.

Yet what draws today's women toward Buddhism is the same impulse women experienced in the past—the wish to be free from suffering. The promise of liberation also remains constant, and contemporary women can still seek nirvana along the same path the Buddha followed. So although contemporary Buddhist women face different challenges and perhaps hold different expectations of how Buddhism can help transform their lives than did their earlier sisters, nonetheless, the practices of love, compassion, and wisdom that are the bedrock of Buddhism are as effective and as relevant today as they have always been.

In some ways culture affects attitudes toward women practitioners more than the passage of time. The early Buddhist women lived in a culture in which women's roles were strictly defined. Thus when they became nuns or yoginis and undertook serious Buddhist meditation, it may have been easier for them to accept that the same cultural limitations applied to their spiritual practice. Contemporary Buddhist women are far less used to gender prejudice. Now that Buddhism has arrived in Western countries, where women have equality with men in many spheres of life, it seems easier for women to be accepted as Buddhist practitioners, as nuns, and as Buddhist teachers.

Yet confusion can occur when a Western woman takes a traditional Asian male teacher. Though the teacher may be a great master and a meditator with deep realizations, he may still have been conditioned by his culture to believe that women are less able or less well suited to serious Buddhist practice than men. Even if this prejudice manifests in subtle or unconscious ways, or is not intentional on the part of the teacher, it comes as a shock to contemporary women and may be hard for them to comprehend. Though some women are strong enough to persevere in their practice over the years and eventually earn the respect of their teacher, others may be affected adversely. For more vulnerable women, assumptions of inferiority may reinforce their lack of self-worth, which is itself a particularly Western psychological phenomenon

There are more lay Buddhist women in the modern world, but Buddhist nuns are still important.

often not understood by Asian teachers. Thus prejudice against women may be different today than it was for early Buddhist women, but its impact can still be negative.

There are, perhaps, more difficult obstacles for Buddhist women today than sexism. Contemporary culture is generally unsupportive of all religious pursuits—witness the general decline in church and synagogue attendance. Society seems focused on the idea of the individual as consumer, rather than as spiritual being. Career development, earning and spending money, buying a home, cultivating a beautiful body, forming relationships, and eventually having children are seen as the path to happiness for modern women, leaving little time for spiritual thought or practice. Unlike early Buddhist women, who often gave up a difficult and limited existence for the relative freedom of spiritual practice, for modern women, ordinary life seems attractive and seductive. Women living in the West seem to be able to have it all these days. Why, most people wonder, would anyone choose to renounce a lifestyle centered around pleasure and material possessions?

Thus women who wish to integrate the Buddha's teachings into contemporary life face new and confusing challenges. Some women, of course, still choose to renounce ordinary life and become Buddhist nuns, who can devote much of their time to meditation, but their number is declining. Most Buddhist women are lay practitioners, who must juggle multiple demands on their time to fit their spiritual practice into a life that includes a job, relationships, and children. Many of these women find that contemporary life makes it difficult to practice meditation seriously in a supportive environment. For some, the only resolution to this conflict is scheduling regular retreats in places dedicated solely to meditation.

Despite these challenges, however, women today have the opportunity to encounter and practice the dharma with an ease undreamed of in earlier centuries. Buddhist teachers, meditation centers, books, video and audio tapes, and the Internet offer Buddhist wisdom from many traditions to all those who are open to learning. With the increasing visibility of Buddhist nuns, female lay practitioners, teachers, and writers, modern Buddhist women no longer need to feel inferior to men or excluded from the dharma. Indeed, contemporary women have many powerful female Buddhist role models from whom to draw inspiration.

In the following stories and interviews, we meet women who have embraced the Buddhist path, each in her own particular way. Though their stories celebrate a diversity of personal interpretations of what Buddhism means today, the women share a commitment to transforming their lives through the Buddha's teachings on awakening. Some have faced enormous difficulties and obstacles; others have renounced material success or the opportunity to have children or relationships; while others report that life has become easier since they embarked on the Buddhist path. Reading their stories allows us to share intimately in the joys and challenges of women whose daily lives help strengthen the current vitality of the feminine face of Buddhism.

Chatsumarn Kabilsingh and the Bhikkhuni Tradition

*My goal is to lead a good life as a nun. I want
to show society that it is possible to live the life
of a renunciant but still be beneficial to society.
We cannot wait for the monks alone to do
the job. We should step forward and offer
ourselves to society.*

—CHATSUMARN KABILSINGH (DHAMMANANDA),

SEEDS OF PEACE

We start with a story that reestablishes a link
between the Buddhist women of many
centuries ago and the modern Theravadan nuns of
Southeast Asia. As we learned in Chapter 1, the
Buddha himself ordained Mahapajapati and her
female companions, making them the first Buddhist
nuns. After the Buddha's death, his teachings spread
first to Sri Lanka, then into the rest of Southeast
Asia. Different schools of Buddhism developed in
these countries, which eventually consolidated into
the Theravada tradition. Later, the teachings spread
to China, Japan, Korea, and other far-eastern
countries, and north to Tibet, where further
developments in Buddhism created the Mahayana
tradition. Though the basic beliefs of the two
traditions are similar, there are some significant
differences in both philosophy and practice.

By the thirteenth century, the Theravadan
Buddhist *Bhikkhu* (monk) and *Bhikkhuni* (nun)
traditions had died out in Sri Lanka. In 1753, the
Sri Lankan Bhikkhu lineage was reestablished, but
not the Bhikkhuni lineage, leaving Buddhist women

in a subordinate position. Over the years many
women and some men have worked toward
restoring the Bhikkhuni lineage, despite resistance
from some conservative bhikkhus and laymen.
Novice Sri Lankan nuns, those who have taken
vows to uphold only ten precepts, were allowed to
travel to Taiwan or Hong Kong to receive full
Bhikkhuni ordination in the Mahayana tradition,
but this compromise solution created much
concern and debate, as Sri Lanka is traditionally
a Theravadan country.

In 1998, an international higher ordination ceremony was organized to take place in Bodhgaya,
India, the place where the Buddha attained enlightenment. Senior bhikkhus from Sri Lanka agreed to
attend along with twenty-two novice nuns, if the
ordination could be conducted according to
the Theravadan tradition as described in the
Cullavagga. This ancient document, or *sutta*,
contains the Buddha's original description of how
women were to receive Bhikkhuni ordination. The
ordination ceremony in Bodhgaya was completed
successfully in the presence of both Mahayana and
Theravada elders. Then the same group attended
another ordination, this one held at Sarnath, near
Varanasi, India, the place where the Buddha first
taught the dharma. At this ceremony, the nuns were
ordained directly by the Sri Lankan bhikkhus. The
final step in the restoration of the Bhikkhuni lineage
in Sri Lanka occurred at the Golden Temple in
Dambulla, Sri Lanka, on the full moon of March
12, 1998. For the first time in hundreds of years,
bhikkhus and bhikkhunis stood together and
ordained novice nuns who had graduated from

their monastic training center. Once again Theravadan bhikkhunis are practicing and participating fully in the Buddha-dharma in Sri Lanka.

Chatsumarn Kabilsingh is from Thailand, another traditional Theravadan country. The Bhikkhuni lineage was never established in Thailand, and women there are generally held in low esteem. Novice Thai nuns, or *maechees*, are considered to be vastly inferior to bhikkhus. Their legal status is also confusing. While the Transport Ministry regards the nuns as lay practitioners and denies them the free travel routinely granted to monks, the Interior Ministry treats them as religious persons and denies them the right to vote. Maechees often end up as servants of the monks, which leaves them little time for spiritual instruction or meditation. If a Thai woman expresses the wish to become fully ordained, she is seen as egotistical. Instead, she is expected to pray to be reborn as a man in her next life! This entire structure of inequality is kept in place by a law that forbids the ordination of bhikkhuni.

Until recently, Chatsumarn Kabilsingh was a professor of religion and philosophy at Thammasat University, Thailand. She is also the author of more than forty books, including the influential *Thai Women in Buddhism*. Her dedication to improving the status of Thai nuns is inspired by her mother, Vorami Kabilsingh, who traveled to Taiwan and took Mahayana Buddhist ordination and then returned to Thailand to found the first Thai

temple for maechees and to devote herself to social work to help Thai women and children. Following in her mother's footsteps, Chatsurmarn has helped to lead the international movement to revive the Bhikkhuni tradition in Thailand and has worked incessantly to redress the inferiority of Thai women in the spiritual sphere.

In February, 2001, Chatsumarn traveled to Sri Lanka to receive the novice *samaneri* ordination, the prerequisite to full Bhikkhuni ordination. Her ordination name is Dhammananda—"joyfulness." She has returned to Thailand and currently teaches at a temple for women. She and other Thai nuns who have been ordained in Sri Lanka remain unrecognized by the Thai Sangha Supreme Council, but the whole issue of the Bhikkhuni order is under review. It is surely only a matter of time before Dhammananda and her Thai sisters are able to receive Bhikkhuni ordination in their own country.

Renate Seifarth

Renate is a former biologist from Germany, who has spent the last twelve years in intensive Buddhist meditation practice. During this period, she has spent a total of five years in retreat. She currently teaches *vipassana* (insight) meditation with an emphasis on how the traditional Asian teachings can be useful in a liberal Western culture. Here is her story, in her own words:

In November, 1988, I asked the manager of a forth-coming vipassana retreat in Bodhgaya, India, "What is it about, a retreat?"

"You will see who you are," he answered.

Fear arose, and I told myself, "If I have fear to know who I am, I better do it."

The fear had good reason. Within a day of silent sitting and walking, I discovered my life had been a series of attempts to overcome feelings of alienation, self-hatred, and unworthiness. No friends, social or political engagement, or different city had had any effect on the cold, closed, merciless heart that seemed at the bottom of my being.

It was my teacher who proclaimed otherwise: "I love you." A sentence that couldn't seem to be true but that was uttered with certainty. Although a profound experience of oneness occurred, I left with no hope but one: knowing this practice would prevent me from ever pretending again that everything is fine if it isn't. It would show me the truth.

Unable to lead a normal life, this seemed to be the only road. I hitchhiked to another retreat in England, only to find the same pain. Piercing, tearing, excruciating pain, but I stayed. Any experience is OK, they said. I experienced relief about not having to be any different from what I was; here was the acceptance I couldn't give myself. Any experience meant also my experience, meant me.

"You mean I am OK as I am?" This was my lifeline, my only hope.

The openness and love I was met with led to a slow shedding of the past; the abuse by my father, my negative beliefs about myself. My ability to trust myself and others grew. During a three-month retreat, I regressed to a toddler stage and reexperienced the sexual abuse by my father. I observed closely how during that early experience I had learned to hate myself. It was a turning point. Painful emotions of self-hatred, alienation, and deep pain started slowly to cease.

A new fascinating interest in the dharma began to grow. Could there even be more to life? What is freedom really? Why would one want to reach Nibbana [nirvana]? Fascinated by a report of a visit to Ajahn Maha Boowa [a well-known teacher in the Thai forest tradition] by one of my teachers, I felt deeply drawn to go and study with him. But this meant Thailand, where I had heard that women were only allowed to stay a limited time and must cook. That's not what I wanted. I, too, wanted to practice like the monks.

Despite those warnings and with the encouragement of my teachers, I took the risk and went. I arrived with a male friend and immediately was ignored by the monks. My friend was offered a stool to sit on, a glass of Coke—but not me. Finally I was led to the women's section. "This is the kitchen."

"Do I have to cook?" I asked immediately.

"No, we just call it that," replied the monk.

But it was a kitchen, as I soon found out. The whole area where women stayed was a kitchen. All women cooked every day to give *dana* [donations] to the monks. Between fifty and a hundred and fifty women cooked for fifty monks. Many lay people also brought food every day, and ninety percent of it left again, so I didn't feel I had to participate.

"The greatest merit comes from practice," my teacher affirmed, supporting me. My women comrades were concerned because I didn't fit in; I didn't behave as a woman when I challenged the monk who was my instructor, telling him how unequally women were treated and how much that hurt. But, "Everyone can get enlightened, and women have the same abilities." These words by Maha Boowa inspired me.

I tried to practice. I lived on a platform with no walls in a tiny bit of original forest full of mosquitos, snakes, scorpions, and ants. It was hot and humid, and at 3 P.M. I would throw some buckets of water over my body. No mattress, no food other than in the morning, no electricity, no washing machines. "One should give up any attachment to pleasure." Was this the freedom I sought?

I was already deeply perplexed, and yet there was this glow in my teacher's eyes, his warmth, humor, lightness, and the impressive stature of Maha Boowa, showing his strength, clarity, and deep compassion. Nibbana: What is this? Why should I want it? In his presence I felt what the lightness that comes from letting go each moment completely could mean. Yes, this I wanted!

Weeks and months passed. The monks built a platform for me, and I was finally accepted by the other women. The question of when I would leave turned into praising comments. A period of letting go followed. First, the body. This body with all its parts could not be mine, and I discovered a greater intimacy and acceptance with the body I had always rejected. Then feelings. I feel, so I am, or I am what I feel, had been my belief. But all the feelings changed and disappeared without trace. A relief; they were just visitors, not me. My mind. For a moment everything was let go of and I discovered a peace that couldn't be any greater. I saw the world with different eyes.

New Year's Eve. I lay on my platform, alone and totally content. But this, too, changed. More women arrived in the monastery and created power struggles between each other. The peaceful environment had gone, and I felt the need to leave. Burma, America. Another two years passed by, and I remained fascinated by the different moves my mind performed. A period of clarity and connectedness was followed by one of dissolution, but only to move on to a deeper awareness of interdependency.

Finally my interest in the world reawakened, the urge to just talk with a good friend, to explore an art gallery, to watch a nice movie. A new stage on this strange journey toward wholeness and freedom began. Instead of just going within, it meant going out, not rejecting pleasure or pain, but embracing both. But another ground carried me.

Helen Tworkov

Best known as the founding editor of *Tricycle* magazine, Helen was born in New York City in 1943. She studied anthropology at Hunter College and City University of New York. From 1964 to 1966, she traveled through Asia, spending most of her time in Kyoto and Kathmandu. She returned to India and Nepal in 1969, but she did not begin meditation practice until 1972. Her first Buddhist teachers were Tibetan. In 1981 she moved into the Zen Community of New York, led by Bernie Glassman. She also studied with Zen teacher Maezumi Roshi from that time until his death in 1995. In 1999, she published *Zen in America*, profiles of five American Zen teachers, and in 1991, she founded *Tricycle: The Buddhist Review*. After ten years at the helm, Helen stopped editing *Tricycle* and became executive director, a position from which she is responsible for the magazine as well as other Buddhist activities.

Recently, I had the opportunity to interview Helen about her experiences at *Tricycle* and about the role and status of women in Buddhism:

Q: *Has your idea of what you wanted* Tricycle *to achieve changed much during the last decade, or is your original vision still a major inspiration?*
A: The original vision was simply to disseminate the dharma. That remains the essential mission and the most inspiring aspect of my work.

Q: *What has been your most interesting experience in working for* Tricycle?
A: I was very unprepared for how complicated this job is. From the very beginning, I quickly learned that it is almost impossible to publish one article that was received favorably by one group but

was not offensive to another. The only neutral ground was with the ancient masters. But part of the mission was to convey that this was for the West, and in the West, and by the West, so to speak. So Buddhists became apt to read the magazine with a kind of internal check list, and with each point, they might say, "I agree with this" or "I don't agree with that." And then in ways similar to people who read the *New York Times* or any news magazine, they like what they agree with, and don't like what they do not agree with. Not very open minded! So I caught onto the fact that our non-Buddhist readership, people who came to the material with no allegiance and therefore no bias, were much more open, and consequently I often found their responses more interesting. They have no agenda to protect and no bias through which material is filtered. So their critiques tend to be more valuable.

Q: Tricycle *is aimed at a predominantly Western audience. What kind of feedback have you had from Asian Buddhist teachers about this orientation?*
A: Well, of course, very few of them read the magazine, either because it is of no interest to them, or because they do not read English. Antagonism toward the magazine in this respect lies with the American Asians. Third and fourth generation Pure Land Japanese American priests, for example, have been very critical of the magazine's almost exclusive focus on so-called "convert Buddhism." There are Tibetan teachers who also do not actually read the magazine but who have, with the aid of their students, arrived at the idea that *Tricycle* "promotes" American, or Americanized or Westernized, dharma. Of course, from a conservative Tibetan view, everything in the West could be perceived as Westernized dharma!

Q: *Buddhism and feminism both claim to be philosophies of liberation. How do you perceive the similarities and the differences between them?*
A: Perhaps this is an old-fashioned and conventional view, but I understand feminism to be a kind of political liberation: liberation from patriarchy and from social structures that create inequality between the sexes. Feminism rests with conventional dualities, and while the goal is equality, there is no attempt to dissolve the dualities themselves. In Buddhism, we work with the relative duality of enlightenment and ignorance. The battle is internal, not external, not dependent on social circumstances or sexual orientation, and any apprehension of the goal necessitates the dissolution of the duality itself.

Q: *Buddhism as taught and practiced in Asian countries has tended to discriminate against women to some extent. How has this affected you personally, and how does* Tricycle *deal with this issue?*
A: I have never understood this issue in terms of dharma, but rather as a social issue in which the dharma structures mirror the society at large, as they do everywhere. How could it be any different? Religion is a social structure. So, no, the social conditions of Buddhism do not dishearten, or discourage, or anger me, any more or less than they do within other aspects of society.

Q: *Do you think that women have changed, or will change, the way dharma is presented and taught?*
A: Yes. At least, I hope so. Most of the religious structures that we know of, in Buddhism as well as other religions, are totally intertwined with patriarchal social systems. So the structures themselves become political, concerned with power, wealth, competition, and with an unchecked interest in "taking over" territory of one kind or another—women, property, countries, whatever. The isolation of women from power structures has provided a different, more marginalized, less power-hungry way of approaching the world, and hopefully this can be put to good use in the evolution of dharma. Of course, we may end up with the Margaret Thatchers and the Indira Gandhis of Buddhism, but my hope is that we cultivate deeper and smaller fields, not get so involved with empire building, and utilize the relatively open communication systems which women often find comforting and men often find threatening.

Ajahn Candasiri

Currently living at Amaravati Buddhist Monastery in Hemel Hempstead, England, Ajahn Candasiri is one of the most senior nuns. I recently had the oppportunity to interview her about her experiences as a Western woman becoming a Theravadan Buddhist nun:

Q: *Could you tell me about your background and how you got involved in Buddhist practice?*
A: I was brought up within the Scottish Episcopal tradition of Christianity. In my teens, I was very devout. I used to like praying and getting up early; I loved the mystery of it all. Later on, I rejected everything to do with organized religion. I went a bit wild at university, being more interested in exploring life itself, not always so skillfully! However, a deep questioning began when a close friend suddenly fell ill. I was very upset by this, but having done everything I could to help her, I was disturbed to notice that, as she was recovering, I began to feel jealous of the attention she was receiving from others.

Fortunately, during this time of deep questioning, I met someone who introduced me to meditation within the Sufi tradition. This gradually led to an exploration of the mystical aspects of several of the major religions, including Islam, Christianity, and Kabbala [the Jewish mystical tradition]. Then, on the recommendation of a friend, an Anglican priest, I began using meditation within the existing framework of the liturgy. I spent time in retreat in Christian monasteries and studied the Gospels, but instead of bridging the gap between my ideals and negative states of mind such as jealousy or worry, these experiences seemed to accentuate it.

During this time I was working in a psychiatric hospital. I could often empathize with people's difficulties, but not having found tools myself to enable a cure for suffering, what I felt I could offer was quite limited. Eventually, by chance, I visited the Hampstead Vihara in London, where I met Ajahn Sumedho. What he said seemed like perfect sense, but I didn't at first realize it was Buddhist teaching. Although the monks looked strange to me, they seemed saner and more comfortable with themselves than anyone I had ever met!

Later, during a ten-day retreat, Ajahn Sumedho spoke about Chithurst, where there would be a monastery for bhikkhus of the forest tradition. He also mentioned the possibility of opportunities for women to train as nuns. Hearing this, I imagined all the women there queuing up to join, but in fact I was the only one! It seemed such a blessing to live wholeheartedly in community with people I respected so much, and I had great confidence in the teaching and practice. I knew I would benefit and sensed that in some way, too, it would help make the world a better place.

Q: *What is your experience of being a Theravadan Buddhist nun?*
A: Well, my experience when I started is very different from my experience now. At first there were just four women living at Chithurst, inspired by Ajahn Sumedho and the other monks. There was a pioneering spirit and, over time, deep affection grew among us; but at first it was difficult. We hadn't chosen to live together and didn't have much in common—apart from being pretty strong-willed! At first we felt very much appreciated by the monks, so it felt fine to serve them and to be, according to the traditional hierarchy, the most junior members of the community. Although the routine and living conditions were harsh, we were contented and happy.

Gradually it became more difficult to accept new novice monks automatically taking their place in front of us. Also, as our numbers grew, it seemed more cohesion was needed. Rather than simply being individuals tacked on at the end of the male community, we needed to be a separate community in its own right. Clearly we were sincere in our commitment, and so Ajahn Sumedho began to sound out the elders of the Sangha in Thailand with a view to offering us a clearer structure within which to practice, something closer to the monks' style of training.

Eventually, after almost four years, it was agreed that a ten-precept ordination could be given involving our relinquishing personal funds. We changed from white to brown robes and were given ceramic alms bowls. Until then, our training had consisted in following the example of the monks as best we could. Apart from regular *dhamma* [dharma] teachings to the community as a whole, there was no formal training for us as nuns. I had never even met another nun!

After working mostly with the monks, I felt very frustrated at first with what seemed like endless discussions that took place in the nuns' community. Then as I reflected that it was part of my *kamma* [karma] as a woman to be with other women, that I couldn't expect to live like the monks, things became easier. I stopped resisting. I became more open to the other women and didn't mind the long meetings any more!

From 1984 till 1991, one of the monks helped us to establish our training. He counseled us and guided us and made the decisions for our community. We all respected him, but as our confidence grew, the time came for us to begin making our own decisions. Personally, I was helped a lot by Maechee Pathomwan, a Thai nun of many years. She encouraged me not to worry too much about getting respect or equality, that these things would arise naturally as a result of the practice. That confirmed an intuition I had had, in spite of others' concern. It was such a relief; it felt so right.

It's always been difficult. We're still learning, and I feel challenged at every level most of the time. Fortunately I have a positive outlook and lots of optimism, even when things look unpromising. I've never had any doubts about our place here, confident that eventually things would come right. It's easy to have an idea of a nuns' community, and it takes a lot of hard inner work to actually make it happen, but I'm convinced it's possible. I feel that this is the best thing I can do with my life, and that brings tremendous joy.

Q: *What is your feeling about the reestablishment of the Bhikkhuni ordination in Sri Lanka?*
A: I think it's great. In some sense, I, too, long to be part of that lineage, going back to the time of the Buddha. In the past, my heart has ached when observing Bhikkhu ordination ceremonies because of the sense that it was something very ancient that we could never be a part of. But then I would consider that in fact we have something very special with our nuns' community. There's the sense of an even greater privilege in opening up a way for women in this tradition. We have our ordination ceremony; we have a community that women can join and practice within. But I would love to take Bhikkhuni ordination before I die!

In regard to reintroducing Bhikkhuni ordination, I do feel some concern about what support is available for those who undertake such an exacting discipline. I know how difficult it can be. So while the thought of women living as bhikkhunis is very inspiring, I feel quite demoralized at the thought of women who have taken Bhikkhuni ordination not being able to live out this training with integrity. For myself, I think it would be important to find an interpretation of the rules that would support us in our aspiration toward liberation. I would also need to know that there was full understanding and approval among the wider sangha.

I sense that it is simply a matter of time. The Rule we follow now is quite similar to the Bhikkhuni *patimokkha* [set of vows], and since there are only about sixteen *siladhara* [ten-precept Theravadan nuns] in the entire world, I feel it would be simpler and less confusing for people if we were bhikkhunis. As it is, people don't quite know what to do with us. Generally we end up with the novices at the end of the line when we visit other communities, which can feel strange!

I feel sad when women struggle to be equal with men. Really, I don't feel that we need to compete. In our monasteries there is a formal respect that we show to the monks, but actually there is a sense of mutual respect and consideration, more a complementary relationship than any sense of rivalry.

Q: *What is the most important thing you have discovered through your practice?*
A: It's really important to enjoy life, to live life fully and enjoy it. For a long while, I was very dutiful and good, but not particularly happy. Now I realize that it's really important to look after oneself and to enjoy life; only then can you really take care of others.

Q: *What advice would you offer those embarking on the Buddhist path?*
A: Don't be afraid of what may come up in the mind. Often people imagine that they are good, kind, patient, and nice, but then when they enter religious training, they discover they are angry, impatient, irritable—not as nice as they thought they were! You don't need to be afraid of that. Instead, take an interest in it. Don't hide anything from yourself. Realize you are more than what you seem to be. Those negative states are just passing phenomena. You don't have to worry about or identify with them.

Q: *Do women have a particular role to play as Buddhism comes to the West?*
A: They can enable a quality of being. Once when I visited Chithurst, there were only monks. There was a macho competitive energy, a hardness, a gung-ho feeling. When a few of us nuns came there, after some days the energy shifted and allowed a softer side to come out in the male psyche. For women in Buddhism, as we find ourselves, develop confidence, and allow the feminine to manifest, it gives a complementary balance.

Jacquie Kilty

Jacquie is a long-time Tibetan Buddhist practitioner and a mother. She lives currently in Devon, England, where she practices as a therapeutic counselor to people in crisis and distressed young people. Here is her story of the years she spent in the Tibetan settlement at Dharamsala, India, current home of the Dalai Lama:

Living with the Tibetan exile community for twelve years without a break [from 1972 to 1984] was a remarkable experience. I grew accustomed to their way of life, their attitudes and day-to-day priorities, and most of all, their religion. The Tibetans were living in this Himalayan province of India as refugees. They had been trickling into India since 1959, the time of the Chinese invasion in Tibet, when India held out its kindly hand to the Dalai Lama and his people.

herbal medicine helped me through the births. It was a joy to have my own children. I used to sit cross-legged at *puja* time [offering ceremonies] with my baby lying on my lap feeding from my breast, or he would sleep or play. I walked with them on my back or hand-in-hand along the rough tracks of the foothills. Nature pervaded and invaded our lives. We listened to Tibetan lamas teach for hours and went shopping in the local Indian and Tibetan bazaars. This was our daily life.

We had no running water in our house; the nearest was a walk through the forest to a spouting pipe in a clearing, where the local sheep, goats, and buffalo drank. Here school children from the local Gaddi village emptied their ink pots at break time and washed their class slates. It was here, too, that I washed our clothes, while Paul and Rohan played close by. But the source of inspiration was the view of the fifteen-thousand-foot mountain above, the enormity of the scenery, and the humble huts that housed the Dalai Lama's meditators halfway up the mountain. This is the scene that will never leave me. I contemplated the teachings of the day here, but at the same time, I watched this extraordinary view and was amongst my daily activities.

My daily trek to the teachings for five years was a long walk below the Tibetan village and down a rough track to the Library of Tibetan Works and Archives. There I listened to Geshe Ngawang, my lama, a strict but immensely learned monk. I had plenty of time to contemplate. Life was at walking pace surrounded by living reminders of the dharma from monks and lay people alike. There was a sense of safety and trust among Tibetans.

There was no doubt that I had embraced the Tibetan philosophy and Buddhism. So, it was only natural that I looked to those women for inspiration, rather than to my own culture, when I became a mother. My only Western friends with children lived way down the mountain. We lived in a pine forest above the Tibetan village at seven thousand feet and were isolated from other families.

The beginnings were romantic. I met Gavin shortly after I arrived in the area. My first pregnancy and birth were extraordinary. The second was much easier and more joyful. Gavin delivered both boys at home, and the gentle and highly revered lady doctor, Dr. Losang Dolma, and Tibetan

My life was basic, no distractions. The essentials were important; nothing unnecessary was achieved nor materially bought. There was birth and death and life in-between.

Our third son was born in a hospital next to the Watford football stadium, north of London. The first match of the season played the night Kim was born. It was very different in England. People spoke the same language and expected certain behavior from you. In India, I had immersed myself totally into motherhood, but back here in England, there were different, external attitudes I had not taken into account. Materials, so many it made me dizzy. How could I decide? There was too much choice, no room for ingenuity or initiative. The washing machine was a press of a button, but what a noise! All that was expected of me, how could I fulfill it? I felt stretched in all directions, exhausted by the bombardment of the senses. Appearances were so important, and there was the feeling of the aloneness of it all. My pillar was my daily practice. Whatever happened, I could sit every day and recollect all that I had learned from the Tibetans and be quiet with my thoughts.

Living in a spiritual community means you are supported by your beliefs. This is evident in parts of the East where it pervades the lifestyle, but material gain is limited. In the West, material support and comfort are in abundance and to be appreciated, but spiritual support is restricted. As the dharma says: Loving kindness starts at home. Then we can include our neighbors and friends, and then slowly this will radiate out to those we meet and beyond, so that our example can permeate life.

Sharda Rogell

Sharda Rogell is an insight meditation teacher. As her story explains, she has spent fifteen years living relatively homeless as a path of renunciation:

How many people start meditation because they are suffering and don't know where else to turn? At twenty-eight years old, I was desperate for help. A friend suggested meditation, and my spiritual journey began with three years of Transcendental Meditation. I moved from the East coast to San Francisco, longing for something more, and took an introductory vipassana meditation class. I knew from the beginning that this practice had the depth I was seeking, so I started sitting longer retreats. After six years of intensive practice, and serving as a retreat cook, I was asked to join Jack Kornfield's first teacher training and began teaching vipassana meditation. Three years later, I turned forty. I had been trying to have a baby for some time but decided to let go of that desire and dedicate my life to the dharma. I decided to leave my marriage and move to England.

The journey has been magical. I have been essentially homeless since I left in 1987. Initially I lived in a Buddhist community in Devon, England, and traveled each winter to Bodhgaya, India, the place of Buddha's awakening, to teach meditation. Fifteen winters in Mother India's spiritual embrace has been my most powerful teacher. Experiencing how eighty percent of the world's population lives by sleeping on straw, eating *chapattis*, rice, and *dal*, living with the simplicity of a backpack, and dealing with my continual resistance to letting go

My life on the road is one of constant letting go. There is little chance of becoming attached to things and people. I have few possessions and live without a fixed income, depending on the generosity of people's donations (*dana*). I travel constantly, spending short visits with people. I could be called a lay renunciate. This way of life has brought about a radical transformation of my heart and mind. I feel little desire for material things or experiences; these feel empty to me now. All that matters is to awaken to Buddha-nature.

I see the strength of the conditioning in my own mind after twenty-five years of committed practice. I know that every living being has the potential to be free from greed, hatred, and ignorance, yet I see how strong the conditioned habit of mind is that prevents overcoming this destructive behavior. Seeing this awakens a deep compassion for myself and others. This clear seeing and openness of heart inspires my teaching and my practice.

Maura Sills

Maura is the founding director of a Buddhist Psychotherapy training program held at the Karuna Institute, in Devon, England. The degree in Core Process Psychotherapy is an M.A. that takes four-and-a-half years to complete. Graduates can be accredited by the Council for Psychotherapy in the United Kingdom.

As Maura explains: "My work over the past twenty years has been to try and embody Buddha-dharma within a training in contemporary psychotherapy. This has been a deep process of learning and continual challenge. The psycho-

of my middle-class comforts and expectations has taught me renunciation and compassion, the cornerstones of Buddha's teaching.

Opening to my own suffering as it arises while coming into contact with the living conditions of the people of India has been my most challenging task. I made close connections in Bodhgaya with the families of my *chaiwalla* (the man who makes and sells tea) and my tailor. This enabled me to witness the hardship of their lives at first hand. I continually asked myself, "Why do I have so much abundance in my life, with education, health, and money, while they have so little?" Our positions could easily have been exchanged. I had to keep letting go into the mystery of these karmic unfoldings.

therapy form of Core Process Psychotherapy is the result of this journey."

Here is Maura's account of her background and experiences in Buddhist practice:

I sat in the meditation room and looked around at those gathered for the short five-day retreat. They were all women; for some reason or other, the men had withdrawn, creating an absence of the embodied masculine. However, inside us all there was a war going on. Two hours before, on a Sunday in October, 2001, America and England had launched air raids on Afghanistan following the terrorist attacks in America on September 11th.

I had decided to tell the retreatants, as they had not had access to the news, so it was with this that we started our silent retreat. The retreat was held within the Buddhist traditions of Theravadan awareness practices, Tibetan awareness, and body-oriented Kum Nye practices. The intention of the retreat was to embody presence at subtler and subtler levels and, within a field of spaciousness, to transform the nature of our experience. Would we be able, individually and collectively, to sit in practice and transform war?

For me as teacher, I was full of responses, reactions, and resonances to the news of yet another war in the world. As always, thoughts and reflections arose. They seemed to distill into "What's important, what matters, what holds meaning, and finally, what can I do?" The enormous privilege of having those five days in a sangha of women who were all engaged in silent practice filled me with gratitude.

What is the place and importance of the feminine in situations of war? Where can I hear the voice of woman's wisdom? Indeed in Afghanistan, for a Westerner, it is difficult to see and hear the presence of women within the process of the politics of that country. What informs and balances the male?

These reflections have a place within Buddha-dharma. When one is part of a spiritual tradition whose teachings were expressed through the male, and the lineages continuing mainly through monks, the same question can be asked. What informs and balances the male face of Buddha-dharma?

My teacher was Taungpulu Kaba Aye Sayadaw [*Kaba Aye* means "world peace"], a forest monk from upper Burma, who spent many years in solitude in a cave. One of his dear students was Rina Sircar. He had known Rina and her family since she was a child. She was ordained as a Buddhist nun when she was very young and was a dedicated disciple of Taungpulu Sayadaw. This forest monk decided to send Rina to America—not to send initially a senior monk, but to send a woman to take the teaching to the West! I am in awe of such wisdom in someone who had so little exposure to any but his own rural Burmese culture and, of course, to decades of practice of Buddha-dharma.

The wisdom of my teacher was to go beyond culture and lineage and to know the importance of the feminine for the West. I experience his insight as both a personal blessing and empowerment and also as a world blessing. I do believe that aspects of the feminine need to be honored and welcomed as equally valuable attributes of human nature, within Buddha-dharma and the world consciousness.

What I have experienced as less present in this world crisis, and also within some of the more male teachings of the dharma, is the embodiment of our ability and capacity to be affected by, and sensitized to, our human condition. To be willing to know our condition deeply and personally, not to settle for concepts and understandings. To go beyond our defensive projections and to fully know the other's suffering as if it were our own. This is true compassion. Only then can equanimity, and the spaciousness within that, allow our nonseparate nature to be experienced. This is mutuality. Then we are prepared to enter directly into relationship with all of life without a sense of position or separate self.

I know these attributes are not known only by women. They, of course, go beyond gender and expand into a larger mind in which there is no gender, no countries, and no enemies. However, they do need to be valued by us all for a wholeness to find expression within Buddhism, within the world.

By the end of the retreat I found that my *metta* [loving kindness] practice had become a direct experience. A genuine and spontaneous feeling of compassion arose in me for all those involved, the apparent victims and perpetrators. However, through the practice, those two positions kept being exchanged. A deep gratitude arose in me for the opportunity to have the profound support of a women's sangha. This opened me up to the wisdom and empowerment of the nonpersonal *tathahta* [suchness] of the feminine face of Buddhism. A privilege to participate in the process of transformation in my small part.

Aung San Suu Kyi

Of the four Buddhist virtues conducive to the happiness of laymen, saddha, *confidence in moral, spiritual, and intellectual values, is the first. To instill such confidence, not by an appeal to the passions, but through intellectual conviction, into a society which has long been wracked by distrust and uncertainty is the essence of the Burmese revolution for democracy.*
—SUU KYI, *FREEDOM FROM FEAR*

We finish this chapter on contemporary Buddhist women with a quick profile of Suu Kyi of Burma. She is an exceptional figure in the modern world who, like the Dalai Lama, is a popular leader of her country but is denied the right to power. Both integrate Buddhist beliefs into the political spectrum and have been awarded the Nobel Peace Prize for their respective efforts to find peaceful, nonviolent solutions to the tragic situations in Burma and Tibet. However, Aung San Suu Kyi is intermittently held under house arrest by the military junta in Burma and is thus unable to speak to the world like the Dalai Lama does from his position in exile.

If Suu Kyi ever leaves Burma, she will never be allowed to return to help her people. Thus she has made the difficult decision to stay. This choice has meant that for many years she has seldom seen her two sons. In 1999, when her husband, Dr. Michael Aris, was dying, and the ruling State Law and Order Restoration Council (SLORC) would not give him permission to visit her in Burma, she made the painful decision not to travel to Britain to be

with him, selflessly putting her country and her people before her family.

Suu Kyi was born on June 19, 1945, the daughter of Burma's national hero Aung San. He had helped liberate his country from British colonialism and from the Japanese attempts to replace the British. Aung San was assassinated by a jealous rival on July 19, 1947, only months before the transfer of power to the fledgling Burmese government which he would have headed. As a result, Suu Kyi has only the faintest memory of her father, yet she has carried on his struggle for a free democratic Burma, a vision inseparable from her Buddhist faith.

After several years abroad, Suu Kyi returned to Burma in April, 1988, to be with her dying mother, leaving her husband and young sons behind in Oxford, England. Later that year, student demonstrations for change, the resignation of General Ne Win, and his announcement of free and fair elections for Burma pushed Suu Kyi to center stage. She quickly emerged as the natural leader and formed the National League for Democracy, which won a landslide victory in May, 1990. But Suu Kyi's party has never been allowed to form a government. For ten years, the SLORC has made no move to relinquish its power, and it seems unlikely that they will ever do so voluntarily.

As a prisoner of conscience, Suu Kyi has endured house arrest, gone on hunger strikes, and kept up attempts at dialogue with the SLORC to achieve a peaceful resolution to Burma's situation. Undoubtedly this part of her life has been overwhelmingly traumatic; yet sustained by her faith, she remains steadfast and committed to her path. Aung San Suu Kyi is a wonderful example of a Buddhist woman living in difficult conditions with inner strength and grace.

In her eldest son Alexander's acceptance speech on her behalf for the 1991 Nobel Prize for Peace, he said: "Although my mother is often described as a political dissident who strives by peaceful means for democratic change, we should remember that her quest is basically spiritual ... she links this firmly to her faith when she writes ... 'Buddhism, the foundation of traditional Burmese culture, places the greatest value on man, who alone of all beings can achieve the supreme state of Buddhahood ... The quest for democracy in Burma is the struggle of a people to live whole, meaningful lives as free and equal members of the world community. It is part of the unceasing human endeavor to prove that the spirit of man can transcend the flaws of his nature.'"

श्रीवाराधमाठवीनमः

CHAPTER THREE
FEMALE BUDDHAS AND BODHISATTVAS

Homage to her who is happiness, virtue, and peace
Who lives in peace beyond suffering,
Who conquers the greatly harmful deeds
With the purity of SOHA and OM.

—*PRAISE TO TARA*

Wisdom Personified

Even in the earliest Mahayana texts, transcendental wisdom is portrayed as a female known as Prajnaparamita. *As she is the Perfection of Wisdom, she is the mother of all the Buddhas. Therefore, in the early Mahayana sutras of Prajnaparamita, she is depicted as a beautiful matriarchal figure. Many scholars wrote prayers to Prajnaparamita, who was also known as the Bodhisattva of Wisdom. She was clearly loved.*

—TENZIN PALMO, *REFLECTIONS ON A MOUNTAIN LAKE*

In this chapter we look at four representative female figures, whose stories, images, and practices help us understand the feminine face of Buddhism. Let's begin with some definitions: *Buddhas* are fully enlightened beings, or literally, "awakened ones" who are liberated from cyclic existence, yet who can effortlessly help those not yet awakened. *Bodhisattvas* are highly realized men and women who are resolved to become enlightened in order to help all beings overcome suffering. They are motivated by the altruistic aspiration to

This community of nuns are participating in a Buddhist ceremony in front of an image of the Buddha, a symbol of their own Buddha-nature, the potential for enlightenment.

free others from suffering, known as *bodhicitta* (the mind of enlightenment). Bodhisattvas take a vow to return again and again to this world to continue helping other beings rather than seeking personal nirvana, freedom from the endless round of rebirths.

The historical Buddha, Shakyamuni, stated quite clearly that both men and women can achieve enlightenment and become Buddhas. Through the centuries, a few highly realized men and women have doubtless done so. However, when it comes to representational forms, there are no female Buddhas. All the historical Buddhas have so far been male. Moreover, the iconographic form of a Buddha is specific, with certain unchanging features, such as how the robe is worn and so on, which seem to allow only for male representation. There are, however, many representations of female bodhisattvas, *dakinis* (sky-dancing spirits of enlightened energy), *yidams* (meditational deities), fierce protector deities, and illustrious women teachers and innovators, some of whom have achieved legendary status.

Though these categories seem to draw clear-cut lines, in Tibetan Buddhism, things are never as simple as they might first appear. For example, Tara is one of the most popular meditational deities. The manifestations of her divine figure are visualized in elaborate Tantric meditation practices as fully awakened Buddhas. Yet Tara's story tells us that she chose not to enter nirvana because of her wish to help all beings attain enlightenment. How, we might wonder, can Tara be both a bodhisattva and a Buddha at the same time? The answer seems to be

Thai nuns meditate on the path to enlightenment. They know that being women is no barrier to awakening.

that in her infinite compassion, Tara manifests as a bodhisattva to continue working for the benefit of others, using the powers of a Buddha to do so. Because of this exceptional altruism, she is described as being the most perfect of bodhisattvas. So, though there are no female Buddha forms, this does not mean there are no female Buddhas. In this chapter we will consider the bodhisattva and meditational deity Tara, the bodhisattva Kuan Yin, the protector deity Palden Lhamo, and the legendary teacher and innovator Yeshe Tsogyal.

Tara

The help provided by Tara was real. She was real; she was divine. Tara was, had always been, and still is the almighty support of her devotees who address her. In fact, she is mightier than Buddhas and Bodhisattvas.

—KEES W. BOLLE, QUOTED IN MARTIN WILLSON, *IN PRAISE OF TARA*

Tara is one of the most popular Tibetan Buddhist deities. Because of her wish to help all beings, she can be many things to many people. Her various names reflect the many roles she plays. Literally, *Tara* means "star," but the name is most often translated as "savioress." Tara saves in that she leads those who wish to attain liberation from the uncontrolled cycle of rebirths known as *samsara* toward the freedom and peace of nirvana. But in a worldly sense, she also saves people from the eight great fears. In ancient India, these dangers were thought of as literal and physical: elephants, lions, snakes, fire, thieves, imprisonment, water (such as floods), and demons. However, the eight fears also have psychological equivalents, perhaps more relevant to us in the modern world. Thus Tara also saves people from the afflictive emotions of elephant-like ignorance; lion-like pride; snake-like jealousy; fiery anger; false views, thief-like stealing of our spiritual development; the prison of greed; the flood of desire and attachment; and demon-like doubts. Buddhism teaches that anyone in any kind of danger or trouble, who prays to Tara with real belief that she can help and with genuine sincerity, can enjoy her divine intervention and assistance.

Tara is also known as the Mother of all the Buddhas and as Prajnaparamita, the Perfection of Wisdom or Knowledge. As such, she is not separate from the true nature of our own mind and the emptiness (*shunyata*) that realizes this nature of mind. Everything that appears to this mind is beyond the duality of subject and object, perceiver and perceived. It is how the Buddhas see. But as we are not yet Buddhas, everything we see appears to exist from its own side. Tara manifests as a deity to help lead us to the experience of nondual perception, so that we can realize emptiness and eventually become enlightened. She exists on both the relative and absolute levels in order to help beings according to their level of understanding. On the relative level, Tara is a savioress and helper in times of trouble; on the absolute level, she is the wisdom mind that brings us closer to enlightenment.

Tara is also the Buddhist manifestation of the universal Mother Goddess, similar in this respect to Kuan Yin (as we shall see later), and is thus an expression of the feminine archetype. Knowing this helps us understand her, as she shares characteristics with Western goddesses such as Demeter, Isis, and Diana, as well as with Indian goddesses such as

This exquisite wall painting of Red Tara is from Tholing Monastery in western Tibet.

Kali and Durga. The all-encompassing Mother Goddess manifests in forms that reflect her various aspects. Green Tara reveals her association with the Earth Goddess, or giver of life, by her green color and by the blue lotus flower or *utpala* she holds in her hand. Another of Tara's forms, White Tara, is associated with the Moon Goddess; luminous white, she sits on a moon disc, with a full moon behind her back. Like the Greek Sophia, Tara is also the Wisdom Goddess of spiritual transformation.

How Wisdom Moon Became Tara

According to stories ... known through the work of Taranatha, a sixteenth-century lama of great realization and scholarship, Tara was a woman before becoming a deity.
—BOKAR RINPOCHE, *TARA THE FEMININE DIVINE*

Many eons ago, the Drum Sound Buddha lived in a world called Multicolored Light. In the royal family among the King's daughters was a princess called Wisdom Moon, who was naturally pious, having great faith and devotion to Drum Sound Buddha. Over the years, she made many offerings to the Buddha and his monks. Eventually she decided she would, in the presence of the Buddha, take the bodhisattva vow, the promise to work toward enlightenment for the benefit of all beings. The monks were greatly pleased by her decision, as she would gain merit from this virtuous action. They suggested that she pray to be a man in future lives, as they believed she would be more useful to others and to the dharma as a man. However, Wisdom Moon had already achieved great realizations, and seeing the narrow-mindedness of this suggestion, she answered from her understanding of the absolute viewpoint:

> *Here no man, no woman,*
> *No I, no individual, no categories.*
> *"Man" or "woman" are only denominations*
> *Created by confusion of perverse minds*
> *In this world.*

She also observed that many men followed the Buddha's path, but few women, and so made the following vow: "As for myself, as long as samsara is not emptied, I will benefit beings appearing in a female body."

She continued her practice and attained enlightenment. On entering a stage of meditation called "concentration that frees beings from samsara," she acquired the name Tara, meaning "savioress" in Sanskrit, and liberated many beings, morning and afternoon. During the time of Buddha Amoghasiddhi in the eon (kalpa) of Perfect Victory, she entered the meditative state known as "concentration that completely vanquishes demons" and helped many beings as soon as they called her name. Because of her quickness in helping beings, she became known as the Swift Courageous Savioress. Tara is also called Daughter of the World's Sovereign, which refers to Avalokiteshvara, the bodhisattva of compassion, as she once manifested from one of his tears, or in some versions of this story, from his heart.

White Tara (Sita-Tara)

White Tara is not a deity different from Tara. There is no separate story recounting her origin, and her activity is only a particular aspect of the protection granted by the deity.

—BOKAR RINPOCHE, *TARA THE FEMININE DIVINE*

Tara has several forms. Her manifestation as White Tara is especially popular because her activity in this form is to provide long life. It is traditional to offer a statue or *thangka* (Tibetan painting on cloth) of White Tara to one's lama or teacher, and Tantric teachers often give White Tara empowerments to their students to authorize them to perform her long-life practices. White Tara is also called Wish Fulfilling Wheel White Tara (*Cinta-mani-cakra Sita Tara*). The following well-known Tibetan story illustrates how White Tara helps her devotees:

A Kadampa Geshe (scholar) awoke one morning remembering a strange but vivid dream, in which the sun rose in the west and set in the east. Feeling disturbed, he went to his lama and recounted the dream, but far from setting his mind at rest, the lama told him that the dream was most inauspicious and was a sign of impending death. The Geshe then went to a palm reader, who confirmed that he had only three years left to live. Realizing the gravity of his situation, the Geshe decided to forego his studies and instead to devote his remaining years to practice.

He visited a lama well-known for his wisdom in giving appropriate practice, explained his predicament, and asked for a practice that would help him to reach enlightenment quickly. However, the lama

told him not to worry and gave him the empowerment of White Tara with instructions to do the practice diligently, promising that in this way, his life would be lengthened. The grateful Geshe embarked on the practice with great energy and soon had a vision of White Tara, who told him he would live to be sixty.

Shortly before his sixtieth birthday, the Geshe turned his mind once again to the deity. White Tara appeared in another vision and told him that if he made a statue of her, he would live another ten years. The Geshe immediately made the statue and continued living in good health. As he neared his seventieth birthday, White Tara asked him to make another statue. The Geshe lived on to see his ninety-fifth birthday before he died.

A modern bronze statue of White Tara from Nepal.

Appearance and Symbolism of White Tara

White Tara represents the fertile aspect of compassion. Countless praises have been written for her by many great Buddhist masters. These prayers describe in much detail her exquisite beauty and tenderness, which demonstrate the pure love and veneration which these masters perceived in the perfect female form.

—ROBERT BEER, *PEACEFUL DEITIES OF VAJRAYANA BUDDHISM* (FORTHCOMING)

The physical form of Tantric deities is always symbolic. The number and color of their faces, arms, legs, objects held in the hands, and other details are meant to call spiritual qualities and ideas to the mind of the meditator. White Tara has one face representing the unified nature of reality and two arms representing the two truths, relative and absolute, that coincide to make up that unified nature. She is described as being as beautiful and youthful as a sixteen-year-old girl, and her white skin is likened to the full moon of autumn. Her divine form radiates the light of five colors—white, yellow, red, green, and blue—representing the spontaneous awareness of the Five Buddha Wisdoms. She has seven eyes, three in her face representing the purity of her body, speech, and mind, and one in each of her two palms and the soles of her feet, representing the four immeasurable qualities of compassion, loving kindness, sympathetic joy, and equanimity toward all beings.

Her right hand is held with its palm open, in the gesture, or *mudra*, of generosity, with which she grants two types of realizations—magical powers, or *siddhis*, and the supreme realization of enlightenment. The thumb and ring finger of her left hand

In this lovely picture of White Tara, her various symbolic attributes are clearly visible— such as the *mudras*, or symbolic gestures, of her delicate hands.

touch in a gesture symbolizing the innate union of the method of compassionate action and the wisdom of realizing emptiness, while the other three fingers of the left hand are extended, representing the Three Jewels: Buddha, dharma (his teachings), and sangha (the spiritual community). The left hand also holds a white utpala lotus flower, showing that Tara has accomplished all realizations and is free from any negativity that needs to be abandoned. Her two legs, which indicate that she is beyond the duality of samsara and nirvana, are in the *vajra* or full lotus posture, showing that she is unaffected by emotional defilements.

Green Tara (Syama-Tara)

Tara's main aspect is that of Green Tara, peaceful, a form with two arms, one face, and two legs. We have seen that her main activity is to protect beings from fear and danger ... Her Green color is that of awakened activity, active compassion ... Green indicates that Tara acts for the benefit of those who pray to her with swiftness of the wind.

—BOKAR RINPOCHE, *TARA THE FEMININE DIVINE*

Green Tara, another of Tara's manifestations, is one of the most accessible Tibetan deities. She is popular among Western Buddhists, especially women, who find her a wonderful and inspirational role model. They pray to Green Tara to help them overcome both worldly and spiritual problems, and many modern practitioners assert that they have experienced her divine assistance. Though she is reputed to dwell with Avalokiteshvara in the Pure Land or "heavenly realm" of Potala, the Pure Land called Harmony of Turquoise Leaves is also attributed to Tara.

In Tibet there are many stories of Tara's paintings and statues speaking miraculously. Tibetans also tell of "spontaneous sculptures," self-created images that appear slowly out of the rock, all by themselves without human intervention. A comparatively recent spontaneous sculpture appeared in Parping, Nepal, just south of Kathmandu, beneath a cave that is famous for its association with Padmasambhava, the eighth-century Tantric master, who spent time there. I have seen this sculpture for myself. A temple has been built around it to protect it, and when visitors enter, temple attendants ensure that the sculpture is not tampered with. My companions and I bought some incense, lit it, and bowed down before the manifestation of Tara. Then we examined it closely and took photographs. The appearance is quite rough, as if the sculpture is still "coming through," but it bears an unmistakable likeness to Tara. Close by, two or three other faint images of Tara appear to be manifesting. It is said that this image is producing itself today in response to the many prayers to Tara that are still being recited.

Here we see the self-manifesting spontaneous sculpture of Green Tara coming through the rock near the cave where Padmasambhava meditated in Parping, Nepal.

Appearance and Symbolism of Green Tara

Through the magic of
     Avalokiteshvara's compassion,
The three times Buddhas' wisdom,
     love, and power
Appear in the lovely form of the
     Goddess of Action
Who saves us all from want—
     at Tara's feet I bow!
—THE FIRST DALAI LAMA, QUOTED IN

MARTIN WILLSON, *IN PRAISE OF TARA*

This early form of Green Tara is called *Khadiravani Tara,* meaning Tara of the Acacia Forest. Khadiravani Tara is shown sitting beneath an asoka tree.

Green Tara has one face and two arms. Her body color is blue-green like an emerald, signifying her awakened activity and her ability to respond compassionately to suffering beings with the swiftness of the wind. She sits with her right leg outstretched, symbolizing her abandonment of all defilements and her readiness to respond to those who call upon her for help. Her left leg is drawn in, showing that she has realized all positive qualities. Her right hand is held palm open, in the wish-granting gesture, and her left hand is held in the gesture of granting refuge or protection. She holds in each hand the stem of a blue utpala lotus flower, symbolizing the fact that all positive qualities have blossomed within her.

Green Tara is adorned with many beautiful jeweled ornaments: a tiara of divine flowers and heavenly jewels, earrings, bracelets, anklets of white pearl and amber, and necklaces of pearl and coral. Collectively, these ornaments show her perfection in the development of method and wisdom. Like White Tara, she is as beautiful and as youthful as a sixteen-year-old girl, symbolizing the perfection of all her qualities. Her straight back shows her diamond-like meditative concentration that never falters. Green Tara smiles sweetly, showing her happy disposition toward all beings, and her charm and beauty reveal her uninterrupted compassion. She is seated upon a moon cushion, symbolizing her fully enlightened attitude, which sits above a fully opened lotus, showing that she is free from all obscurations.

Though White Tara and Green Tara are Tara's two main forms, traditionally there are twenty-one manifestations of Tara, as well as eight Taras who offer protection from the eight fears. A meditation practice based on Red Tara (*Rigjed Lhamo*) has recently come to light. The practice was "discov-ered" in the twentieth century by Apong Terton, a lama of the Nyingma lineage. A *terton* is a spiritual treasureseeker, who brings to light hidden teachings and practices called *terma*. The Red Tara terma emanated originally in the mind of Amitabha Buddha. Eventually, the lineage passed to the eighth-century Tibetan Tantric master Padmasambhava. He instructed his consort Yeshe Tsogyal to conceal the teachings as hidden treasures to be discovered at the appropriate time to be of most benefit to humanity. The practice of Red Tara, called the "Treasure Cycle of Red Tara," is taught mainly by contemporary Nyingma lama Chagdud Tulku Rinpoche in his dharma centers in California and Brazil. The transmission of a new Tara practice in the West and in our time shows that Tara is not just an historical or mythical figure, but manifests as a living compassionate presence for us today.

Praise to Tara

The "Praise to the Twenty-One Taras" is one of the most commonly used Tibetan Buddhist prayers. In Tibet, many simple and sometimes illiterate lay people can recite it by heart. Today it is used as part of the practice in many Western Buddhist centers. A full understanding of the praise would require extensive commentary and a familiarity with Tantric practice. However, you can simply recite the excerpt from the prayer quoted below with faith in Tara's compassionate help and protection, remem-bering that she has vowed to help all beings. The first verse incorporates Tara's mantra, which can also be recited on its own:

OM TARE TUTTARE TURE SOHA.
OM, homage to the sovereign,
the noble, the liberating one.
Homage to TARE, the swift,
the courageous one.
In front of you, who with TUTTARE
dissipates all fears,
In front of you, who with TURE
provides all benefits,
In front of you, SOHA, I bow down.

Homage to the liberating one,
swift and courageous,
Whose sight is like instant lightning,
Who arises from myriad stamens
Of the lotus face of the
Protector of the three worlds.

Homage to her whose face gathers
One hundred autumn full moons,
Who blazes with the sparkling light
Of a thousand stars.

Homage to her whose hand is adorned
With a blue and gold water-born lotus,
Who has for her domain giving, effort,
Asceticism, peace, patience, and concentration.

Homage to the Crown of the Blessed One,
To her who enjoys the infinite and victory,
Who is trusted by the Children of the
Conquerors
Who have achieved all perfections ...
—BOKAR RINPOCHE, *TARA THE FEMININE DIVINE*

Kuan Shih Yin

*Although the bodhisattva is the embodiment of compassion, cultures have made
different choices in representing him/her. China and countries having historical and cultural
connections with her ... identify Kuan Yin as the exemplar of wisdom for meditators
and the "Goddess of Mercy," who is particularly kind to women.*

—CHUN-FANG YU, *KUAN-YIN: THE CHINESE TRANSFORMATION OF AVALOKITESHVARA*

Like Tara, Kuan Yin is a great bodhisattva, a compassionate goddess and a savior of all who call upon her for help. Her full name is Kuan Shih Yin, which means "she who listens to the cries of the world." She both leads Buddhist practitioners toward enlightenment and helps everyone who prays to her to overcome their worldly problems. Kuan Yin evolved in China from the Indian bodhisattva of compassion known as Avalokiteshvara. Because Avalokiteshvara is male, we might wonder: How did Kuan Yin transform into several female forms, and why? As we will see in Chapter 5, artistic representations of Kuan Yin can help us trace her transformation from male to female form. However, let's begin by looking at Kuan Yin's various manifestations, the legends and tales surrounding her, her significance in Chinese Buddhism and culture, and her influence today.

Avalokiteshvara, the male bodhisattva who represents compassion, was first brought to China by traveling monks as early as the first century C.E., some five hundred years after the Buddha's death. The first indigenous Chinese form of Kuan Yin to appear was Water Moon Kuan Yin. Though some earlier male forms of the bodhisattva had moustaches, Water Moon Kuan Yin had a smooth face and androgynous features. These subtle changes helped the bodhisattva transform from male to female form. Indeed, from the tenth century onward, Kuan Yin was increasingly depicted in China as a woman. The first feminine form to appear is known as White Robed Kuan Yin. Though similar to the male Water Moon Kuan Yin, this figure is clearly female. This iconographic change was supported by various legends and miracle tales of the time that mention a "woman in white," who miraculously appeared to those in need of help. White Robed Kuan Yin wears her robe over her head in the hooded style of Chinese women of that period, which reinforced her connection to the people and made her broadly accessible.

The *sutras* (Buddhist scriptures) do not recount Kuan Yin's transformation to female form. Though the texts do mention Avalokiteshvara/Kuan Yin as manifesting in various forms, male and female, to help sentient beings, the classical texts universally depict the bodhisattva as male. Because the feminine forms of Kuan Yin do not follow the scriptures, it seems clear that they developed alongside the traditional sutras, supported by later Chinese texts, legends, and miracle tales. Sometimes Kuan Yin devotees had spontaneous visions of the bodhisattva.

Kuan Shih Yin is shown here in the form of White Robed Kuan Yin. She is seated upon a rock at the entrance to her ocean cave on the island of P'u-t'o shan, a famous site of pilgrimage for Kuan Yin devotees.

It is likely that some of these visions were described to artists and sculptors. These firsthand accounts initiated subtle changes in the artist's depictions, some modifications unconsciously reflecting the Chinese cultural background; others arising from the artist's attempts to recreate faithfully the vision of the person who commissioned the work. It seems clear from this evidence that the Chinese conception of compassion had female qualities.

Kuan Yin was able to bring a simple form of Buddhist practice to the masses of ordinary, often uneducated, Chinese women and men. Since Kuan Yin was not confined to the male temples and monasteries, people could worship and pray to her directly without the necessity of requesting a monk to recite a sutra or perform a ceremony. In this way, Kuan Yin became an authentic presence through her encounters with real people, beyond the mythical figure described in the sutras. As a result of her popularity, some of the prayers to Kuan Yin came to have a worldly focus. People prayed for children, especially boys; for safety generally and when traveling; and for wealth and prosperity. In this more worldly sphere, Kuan Yin was often referred to as the Goddess of Compassion, the Goddess of Fertility, and the Goddess of Mercy. Since no other Chinese deity possessed both divine and worldly characteristics, and because she was a new and exotic figure, Kuan Yin was unparalleled in capturing the popular imagination. From China, worship of Kuan Yin spread to other Asian countries. In Japan, she is venerated as Kannon or Kanzeon; in Korea, she is called Kwanse'um; and in Vietnam, she is called Quan-am.

Legends About Kuan Yin

The central and most popular legend about Kuan Yin tells of Princess Miao-shan, whose name means "wonderful goodness."

Princess Miao-shan was the youngest of three daughters of King Miao-chuang. Since the king had no sons, it was the duty of daughters to marry.

The King expected that one of his sons-in-law would demonstrate the qualities of a ruler and become his heir. From an early age, Miao-shan was inclined to Buddhist practice. She kept a vegetarian diet, read the scriptures, and practiced meditation diligently. When she reached the age of marriage,

Kuan Yin evolved from the male bodhisattva of compassion, Avalokiteshvara, known as Chenrezig in Tibet. This picture of four-armed Chenrezig is by a Western artist.

Miao-shan refused to obey her father and take a husband. The King became incandescent with rage, as it was almost unheard of for a daughter to disobey, and he decided to punish the girl harshly.

Miao-shan was imprisoned in the palace gardens and forced to perform manual labor. Everyone expected she would fail and give in to her father's wishes, but seeing her distress, the gods helped her complete her work. The King then tried another ruse and allowed Miao-shan to go to the White Sparrow Nunnery, in the belief that she would turn away from the harsh life of a nun. However, Miao-shan proved to be even more sincerely religious than the nuns. In a fit of rage, the King had the nunnery burned to the ground with five hundred nuns inside and ordered the execution of his disobedient daughter. However, the gods intervened again, and after Miao-shan's soul had visited hell and preached compassion to the suffering beings there, she returned to her worldly body.

Desiring a quiet place to meditate in peace, Miao-shan traveled to the remote, mountainous area of Hsiang-shan, where she meditated for nine years and became enlightened. Meanwhile, the King had become seriously ill with a mysterious disease that seemed incurable. When Miao-shan learned of her father's illness, she disguised herself as a monk, traveled to the palace, and pronounced that only medicine made from the eyes and hands of a person who had never felt anger could cure him. She then predicted where such a person could be found and returned to Hsiang-shan. When the King's servants followed her directions and arrived in Hsiang-shan, Miao-shan gouged out her own eyes and cut off her

hands and offered them freely. After partaking of the medicine made from these offerings, the King recovered completely. He then went on pilgrimage to thank his mysterious savior. When he saw the handless and eyeless hermit, he recognized his daughter and was overcome with remorse. The entire royal family converted to Buddhism and begged Miao-shan to give them instruction. After doing so, Miao-shan transformed into Thousand-Eyed and Thousand-Armed Kuan Yin and ascended to the Heavens, finally leaving her human form. The newly devotional King decreed that a temple be built at the place of her ascent to honor her.

This popular story, with variations and embellishments, is embedded in Chinese folklore. However, the legend functions as more than a folk tale. It establishes Kuan Yin as a bodhisattva who demonstrates the Perfection of Giving (Sanskrit *dana*), one of six perfect actions performed by bodhisattvas. (The other Perfections are Patience, Morality, Joyful Effort, Concentration, and Wisdom.) Only a highly realized bodhisattva can give of his or her body purely without attachment or aversion. A popular story tells of a previous incarnation of the Buddha, who gave his body to a starving tigress so that she might feed her cubs. Miao-shan's sacrifice is no less noble. The story also helped popularize the somewhat exotic form of Thousand-Eyed and Thousand-Armed Avalokiteshvara and bring it firmly into Chinese Buddhist culture. An early statue of Kuan Yin in this form once stood at the gateway to the Buddhist monastery at Hsiang-shan.

Miracle Tales of Kuan Yin

A mind perfected in the four virtues,
A gold body filled with wisdom ...
Her green jade buttons
And white silk robe
Bathed in holy light ...
—WU CH'ENG-EN, QUOTED IN CHUN-FANG YU,
KUAN-YIN: THE CHINESE TRANSFORMATION
OF AVALOKITESHVARA

The legend of Princess Miao-shan's metamorphosis into Kuan Yin transforms the mythical figure of the bodhisattva into an historical person, complete with a life story. All Chinese gods receive great homage on their birthdays. Kuan Yin's is celebrated on the nineteenth day of the second Chinese month, the date Miao-shan is reputed to have become Kuan Yin. It is customary at this time for devotees to make a pilgrimage to one of the many temples, monasteries, or holy places associated with Kuan Yin. The most famous of these is P'u-t'o Shan, a small island just off the south coast of mainland China. This place is considered to be one of the four sacred Buddhist mountains of China. P'u-t'o Shan is thought to be the Chinese Potalaka, the island home of Kuan Yin described in the sutras. There Kuan Yin sometimes miraculously appeared to pilgrims in a place called the Cave of Tidal Sounds. Such appearances are among the many "efficacious wonders" in the miracle tales about Kuan Yin.

One typical story of this kind is set in the twelfth century. Huang Kuei-nien and some companions undertook the pilgrimage to P'u-t'o Sha. They went

This Chinese statue of Kuan Yin radiates a divine, otherworldly presence, and is seen by Buddhists to embody the compassionate qualities of the bodhisattva.

to the Cave of Tidal Sounds and prayed with great devotion, chanting the name of Kuan Yin. Suddenly they saw a brilliant light, and Kuan Yin appeared, sitting on a rock above the cave. So moved was Huang that he vowed to dedicate his life to studying the Buddhist scriptures, eating only a vegetarian diet, and refraining from killing.

A more modern tale is related by the respected authority on Kuan Yin, Chun-Fang Yu. As a child, she heard many tales about the wonderful bodhisattva Kuan Yin from her grandmother, who was a pious devotee. When Chun-Fang was eight, World War II had recently ended. Her family, which had been displaced by the turmoil of the war, had been waiting in Wuhan near the River Yangtze for three months to secure seats in a boat to take them home. The day finally came for the family to embark on their journey. As they were waiting on the river bank to board the boat, the grandmother suddenly insisted they not go. She had seen a vision of Kuan Yin standing in the river, gesticulating that they should remain where they were. Very reluctantly, the family gave in, thinking that the old woman was full of superstitious nonsense. However, shortly after leaving the shore, the boat hit mines that had been left by the departing Japanese army and it sank, with much loss of life.

This story shows how faith and devotion to Kuan Yin can still bring about miracles in modern times, despite our scientific skepticism about such events. In this way Kuan Yin remains a powerful and effective Buddhist refuge. If she can bring about worldly benefits, then, out of her great compassion, she can also help us on the path toward enlightenment.

A Visualization of Kuan Yin

A popular way to worship Kuan Yin is to visualize her. An old nun living during the early part of last century in Ta Fu Szu Monastery in Canton had experienced a miraculous intervention by Kuan Yin in her own life and was devoted to her. She described her practice to the late John Blofeld, a renowned Buddhist scholar:

"At first you understand, Sir, I just recited Her name. It wasn't enough. I wanted to see her. So I asked at the temple in K'ai Ping how it could be done. A monk there taught me a fine method ..."

Here is my paraphrase of the visualization, which we can easily practice today:

Find a quiet place outside, preferably a hill top, where there is an unobstructed view of the sky. If this is not possible, then sit facing a blank wall as is done in the Zen tradition. Using the mind, make everything appear empty, so nothing is there. Then visualize the sea, with a full, white moon in a blue black sky risen over the sea, made silver in the moonlight. Focus your concentration on the moon for a long time, trying to feel calm and happy. Then the moon slowly becomes smaller, until it is the size of a pearl, but brighter at the same time so that it becomes almost unbearable to look at. Slowly the pearl starts to grow and transforms into Kuan Yin, dressed in glistening white and standing against the night sky upon a lotus floating on the waves. There is a halo around her head and her body, and the image is clear and bright. Kuan Yin is smiling at you. She is so happy to see you that there are tears of joy in her eyes. Keep your mind calm, and quietly recite her name under your breath for as long as you can hold the visualization. Eventually Kuan Yin disappears by getting smaller until there is only empty space left, not even a sense of self, just emptiness. Rest in the emptiness as long as you can before returning to daily life. (Adapted from John Blofeld, *In Search of the Bodhisattva of Compassion*)

Palden Lhamo

Symbolically, Palden Lhamo is one of the most fascinating and complex of Buddhist deities.
Her extremely wrathful form embodies all that is fearful and horrific in the human psyche,
combining the necromancy of the charnel grounds, the magic ritualism of Indian Tantra, and the
violence of the battlefield. Her indestructible wrath overcomes all malice, hatred, and aggression,
and as the Great Mother, she protects her devotees from all corruptions, negativities, and curses.
—ROBERT BEER, *WRATHFUL DEITIES OF VAJRAYANA BUDDHISM* (FORTHCOMING)

The wrathful goddess Palden Lhamo came to Tibet from India and was originally a ferocious demoness. When Padmasambhava came to Tibet from India in the eighth century, Tibetan King Trisong Detsen gave him the task of subjugating the local spirits, who were opposing the king's establishment of Buddhism as the state religion. According to legend, Padmasambhava "tamed" Palden Lhamo and bound her to an oath to protect the dharma. In the fifteenth century, the First Dalai Lama made Palden Lhamo his main personal protector. In the seventeenth century, the Great Fifth Dalai Lama had many visions of Palden Lhamo, which caused her to rise to great prominence. Subsequently she became the main protective goddess of Tibet. The name Palden Lhamo, or *Sri Devi* in Sanskrit, means "glorious goddess." She is also known as *Remati*, meaning "great mother." In her main form described below, she is known in Tibetan as *Magzor Gyalmo*, which means "the queen with magical powers to repulse armies."

In one of the many legends surrounding Palden Lhamo, she was cursed by her mother to be extremely ugly and to have poisonous breath that spread pestilence and plague. The curse also gave Palden Lhamo a black complexion, sagging breasts, a protruding belly, and thin limbs, which is how she is depicted. Palden Lhamo rides upon an iron mule with wings of wind across an ocean of blood. The mule has three eyes, one of which is in the left rump. The two eyes on the mule's face gaze to the present and the past, while the eye in the rump looks to the future. The mule has a bridle and saddle girth made of ferocious hissing snakes, and the saddle is made of the flayed skin of Palden Lhamo's son, who was a cannibal. The mule is led in the front by a crocodile-headed goddess called Makaravakra and followed by a lion-headed goddess called Simhavakra. These two goddesses are mental projections of Palden Lhamo. She is also accompanied by a retinue of millions of black creatures and demonesses.

Her dark blue body is covered in sesame oil; her tawny hair blazes upward; she wears a crown of five dried skulls and a necklace of fifty freshly severed human heads. She has three round, red, angry eyes; a human corpse is laid across her mouth. A lion arises from her right earring and a snake from the left. She wears an upper robe of black silk, a scarf of flayed human skin, a lower

The Tibetan Buddhist wrathful deities, such as Palden Lhamo depicted here, appear horrific, but their symbolism is concerned with transforming negative emotions into their positive, enlightened counterparts.

holds in front of her heart the skull of a child born of incestuous union. The skull is full of magical "charm" blood. She bears five magical weapons, comprising a pair of divination dice, a bundle of red curses, a sack of contagious diseases, a ball of variegated magical thread, and a wooden tally-stick inscribed with magical designs to nullify curses. She is surrounded by a storm of green winds with blazing sparks.

As Robert Beer reminds us, wrathful figures like Palden Lhamo appear horrific because the negative mind states and other obstacles they have sworn to destroy are, if anything, even more terrible. The wrath of such deities and protectors is, therefore, directed not against us, but against the forces of hatred and aggression that can threaten our safety, destroy our peace of mind, and block our spiritual progress. Palden Lhamo's horrific attributes are symbols of the darkest side of human nature, which she manifests in order to transform the negative defilements of anger and hatred into

robe of tiger skin, and broken chains around her ankles. The sun blazes from her navel, a crescent moon crowns her head, and above her head is a canopy of peacock feathers. In her right hand, she wields a red sandalwood club, and her left hand

their positive counterparts of compassion and wisdom. Thus although her appearance may at first seem frightening and repulsive, Palden Lhamo is ultimately as compassionate and as wise as Tara. As the patron mother goddess of Tibet, Palden

Lhamo functions to protect the land from invasion, the people and their spiritual practice from degeneration, and the precious dharma from impurity and corruption.

When His Holiness the Fourteenth Dalai Lama fled from Tibet on the evening of March 17, 1959, he could take very little. One important and sacred object he did take on his flight into exile in India was an ancient, rolled-up thangka of Palden Lhamo that had belonged to the Second Dalai Lama. It is said that the Dalai Lama always has this thangka with him, even when he travels. So, it seems that Palden Lhamo still plays a major role as a protector deity for the Dalai Lamas and for Tibetan Buddhism.

His Holiness the Fourteenth Dalai Lama.

Palden Lhamo is important in another way as well, as an expression of a valuable aspect of the feminine in Buddhism. Told that it is not "feminine" to be angry or violent, women are often encouraged to deny, hide, or suppress their wrathful and negative energies. Sadly, many women repress these feelings in damaging, unbalanced, and unskillful ways. Although obviously women—and men—do not want to cultivate the expression of negative emotions, they do need to learn how to transform them skillfully. If women simply bottle up their anger and violent feelings, these emotions may lurk in the shadow of their psyches, only to spring out later in unexpected and inappropriate ways. Palden Lhamo offers a feminine wrathful vision that women can use in Buddhist practice to help them transform their negative emotions while still honoring the power behind them. This power and energy can then be used to cultivate positive qualities such as compassion.

Praise to Palden Lhamo

The following praise to Palden Lhamo is by the sixteenth-century lama Taranatha, from his treatise *Rin-jung Gyatsa*, meaning "Mine of Jewels." The *Rin-jung Gyatsa* draws from an important Buddhist text that is a compilation of *sadhanas*, or ritual practices, based on all of the main meditational deities.

> *Great goddess of the desire realm,*
> *your form is glorious.*
> *Riding upon a mule that traverses*
> *five hundred leagues in an instant,*
> *Holding your symbols of the*
> *magnificent club and a skull,*
> *Wearing a tiger hair apron,*
> *a scarf, and serpent skirt.*
> *The sun is in your navel,*
> *the moon adorns your crown.*
> *Resplendent Queen of Realm,*
> *mistress of blood diseases,*
> *I praise you goddess Remati.*
> *Please your fulfill your appointed task,*
> *O great yogini.*
> —QUOTED IN MARTIN WILLSON, TRANS.,
> *DEITIES OF TIBETAN BUDDHISM*

Yeshe Tsogyal

*Her name was Yeshe Tsogyal, and in the cult that grew up around her
and her Guru [Padmasambhava], she became the Guru Dakini, the Sky Dancer,
the embodiment of the female Buddha.*

—KEITH DOWMAN, *SKY DANCER*

Yeshe Tsogyal was born during the reign of Tibetan King Trisong Detsen. During her birth, the lake near her parents' house increased significantly in size, which was taken to be a most auspicious sign. The baby girl was thus named *Tsogyal*, meaning "Queen of the Lake." From an early age, she displayed great intelligence, strong spiritual inclination, and a phenomenal memory, which later on allowed her to remember all of her Guru's teachings.

Yeshe Tsogyal was also a great beauty, causing her two main suitors to be prepared to fight over her. Ignoring her wishes to live a celibate and spiritual life, her father told her that she must accept the first of her admirers to grab hold of her. When both suitors were camped nearby with their retinues, her father sent Yeshe Tsogyal outside. When she refused to accept the advances of the successful man, she was beaten cruelly until her back was a river of blood. She escaped and was hotly pursued. When the king learned of this disgraceful behavior, which was causing distress and division among his subjects, he decided to marry Yeshe Tsogyal himself. Seeing her obvious faith and devotion to the Buddhist teachings, he appointed her custodian of the dharma and arranged for Buddhist teachers to instruct her further.

Trisong Detsen was himself a devout Buddhist. He invited the great Guru Padmasambhava to his palace and requested teachings that would lead him to enlightenment. When Padmasambhava agreed to introduce the king to the Tantric teachings, the king offered him Yeshe Tsogyal to be his consort as an expression of his gratitude. Although Trisong Detsen wished to make Tibet a Buddhist country, there were many *Bon* (the original shamanic spiritual tradition of Tibet) ministers at his court who were furious at the king's action. Fearful of retribution against the king, Padmasambhava and Yeshe Tsogyal fled to remote Terdrom and practiced Tantric yogas in a cave. This cave, which became known as *Tsogyal Sangpuk* or "Tsogyal's secret cave," can still be visited today as a pilgrimage site.

Padmasambhava, also known as Guru Rinpoche, had many consorts, among them the spiritually accomplished Indian Princess Mandarava, but Yeshe Tsogyal was his main disciple. She spent many years doing the most austere practices in harsh and remote locations. When she eventually attained Buddhahood, Yeshe Tsogyal had many disciples herself who were devastated at losing their guru. She replied to their pleas for her to remain:

O pity! Listen you faithful,
    sad Tibetan people!
This Supreme Being is the Dakini
    Queen of the Lake of Awareness!
My defiled body has been absorbed
    in immaculate inner space,
And I am a Buddha in the lotus-light
    of dynamic space;

I tell you, you need not be anxious, be happy!
People of Tibet afflicted with infinite anxiety,
Laden with behavior patterned
    by negative karmas,
When you see that your personal pain
    is self-inflicted,
The Three Jewels are your refuge from suffering.
—QUOTED IN KEITH DOWMAN, *SKY DANCER*

Yeshe Tsogyal is famous for remembering all of Padmasambhava's teachings. She is reputed to have lived for two hundred years after Padmasambhava's death, which we can interpret as "a very long time." During this later part of her life, she wrote down many of his teachings and hid them in the form of treasures (*terma*) so that they might be discovered centuries later and be revealed to future generations in need of them. Terma can be hidden in rocks, trees, and sacred lakes, but also in the minds of beings, and as we saw in the case of the Red Tara practice, some are occasionally still revealed today.

The Legacy of Yeshe Tsogyal

My body became a sky-dancing rainbow body.
—YESHE TSOGYAL

Yeshe Tsogyal's legend, which wonderfully combines history and myth, is inspirational for women practicing Buddhism today. We see Yeshe Tsogyal overcoming the dreadful behavior of her father and suitors to become a revered yogini and teacher, finally attaining enlightenment. She accomplishes this through the particular Buddhist practice of Tantra, which does not appeal to all Buddhists, though it does have a particular relevance to women. One of the Tibetan words for woman is *kyemen*, meaning "inferior birth," which reflects to some extent the limited opportunities for Tibetan women in both worldly and spiritual pursuits.

Padmasambhava, also called Guru Rinpoche, is seen accompanied by Yeshe | Tsogyal at the bottom right, and by Mandarava, his Indian consort, at bottom left.

However, when Yeshe Tsogyal was describing the difficulties of being a woman practitioner in a patriarchal society to Padmasambhava he replied:

The ground of Liberation
Is this human frame,
        this common human form—
And here distinctions, male and female,
Have no consequence.
And yet if bodhicitta
        [the mind of enlightenment] graces it,
A woman's form indeed will be supreme.
—QUOTED IN KEITH DOWMAN, *SKY DANCER*

Padmasambhava's answer points to the teaching that in Tantra, the power of the practice can turn even the most overwhelming obstacle into the fruit of the path. Indeed, problems can be considered a blessing because they help us learn to let go of ego and suffering and to realize that nothing is permanent. We can see this principle at work in our own lives, as well in as our Buddhist practice. Whenever we overcome some great difficulty or survive some trauma, we have the opportunity to learn from our experience and to gain wisdom. If we do manage to gain something positive from our adversity, we say we are better or stronger for having had the experience. In Buddhism, wisdom is considered to be female, while compassion is male. Working with this essentially female wisdom through their psychology, emotions, and supposedly lesser female body, women are graced with a wonderful potential to transform their suffering into the path leading to enlightenment.

CHAPTER FOUR
WOMEN BUDDHIST TEACHERS

*The task of a teacher is to empower
you, to wake you up to your own inner
teacher. The true teacher works to
make himself or herself redundant.
And life itself is the supreme teacher...*

—MARTINE BATCHELOR

Women of Wisdom

If being a woman is an inspiration, use it.
If it is an obstacle, try not to be bothered.
—VEN. KHANDRO RINPOCHE, QUOTED IN JUDITH
SIMMER-BROWN, *DAKINI'S WARM BREATH*

A group of Buddhist nuns studying. Through dialogue with Westerners, the Dalai Lama is encouraging more Tibetan nuns to train to become teachers.

Ven. Khandro Rinpoche, quoted above, is one of few female Tibetan Buddhist teachers; she is highly regarded by Tibetans and Westerners alike. Over the last few years, His Holiness the Dalai Lama has encouraged the establishment of additional nunneries and the development of structured teaching programs for nuns, with the aim of training more women as Tibetan Buddhist teachers. These actions are partly in response to dialogues with Western Buddhists about the scarcity of traditionally trained women Buddhist teachers. While it is true that female teachers in Asian Buddhist countries have been exceptional and rare, a strong and inspirational female presence has always come through in other ways, in stories, folk tales, and myths, and through the roles women have played in the biographies of the great Buddhist saints.

In this chapter we look at the representation of women in Buddhist stories and see how these tales sometimes reveal subtle or hidden teachings, beyond the more obvious purpose of the story. Feminine Buddhist wisdom is contained and celebrated in stories in which women demonstrate great faith, compassion, or wisdom. However, the selection here is only part of the canon of Buddhist stories and, in its fuller context, must be seen to exist alongside other tales that reinforce negative stereotypes of women as being stupid, idle, promiscuous, or simply irrelevant. In the second half of the chapter, we hear from three of the most important contemporary female Buddhist teachers, one from each of the three main Buddhist traditions, who speak candidly about the question of modern women teaching and practicing the dharma.

The Lama and the Old Woman

In this often-told Tibetan folk tale, a wise old woman bestows a teaching in an indirect but skillful way:

A famous lama came to teach at an old woman's local temple. The pious old woman wanted to make a significant offering to the lama, so she prepared a kilo of fresh yak butter, a highly valued commodity used to make Tibetan tea, and then went along to the temple. The lama gave a lengthy initiation to the huge throng gathered there. At the end of initiations, it was customary for participants to file past the lama and receive a blessing, bestowed by the lama touching each person's head with a sacred nectar-filled vase. As there were so many people in attendance, the lama decided that he would instruct them to visualize receiving this blessing instead. The old woman duly visualized the blessing and completed the initiation ceremony. At the end of the rite, when participants would usually make offerings to the lama, the old woman stood up. In a voice not dissimilar to the lama's, she said: "Now, venerable lama, please visualize yourself as having received this offering of fine yak butter you see me holding here." The wise old woman then made her way home, clutching her butter and chuckling quietly.

In this tale, as in several in the Tibetan tradition, the wise old woman—a well-known archetype straddling many cultures—bestows a teaching through her observations and actions. Though the lama was tired, the ceremony long, and the audience vast, he should have made the extra effort to give the blessing to each person. By wittily pointing out this failing, the old woman shared her wise insight with all present without being overtly disrespectful to the lama. There are several Buddhist stories in this mode. Such tales show respect for the natural wisdom of "wise old women," who are often mothers, usually uneducated, yet who have achieved realizations through simple practices such as repeating mantras and making prostrations with deep faith, love, and devotion.

These folk tales function to maintain the status quo. They do not pose a threat to the patriarchal religious hierarchy, yet they allow feminine wisdom to have its say. Indeed, the natural wisdom of the mother is embraced in Buddhist culture, which venerates both maternal love and kindness and the wisdom that comes with age. Tibetans are not adverse to poking fun at those in high positions when their clarity and wisdom do not shine through their behavior. In a way, the central teaching of this tale is that Buddhist wisdom can come from anywhere, even from unexpected places; it is not just found sitting on a lama's teaching throne. This message roots Buddhism firmly in everyday life and in the natural wisdom of ordinary people like the old woman. It makes clear that a simple old woman can sometimes be as wise as a high lama.

The Nun Who Did Not Succumb to Love

This story from the Zen tradition turns a stereo-typical view of women neatly on its head:

In a Japanese monastery, twenty monks and one nun, whose name was Eshun, were studying Zen Buddhism and practicing meditation with their Zen master. Eshun was very beautiful, even with her head shaved and wearing robes, a fact that did not go unnoticed by several of the monks. One of this group of admirers became so infatuated with Eshun that he wrote her a love letter requesting that they meet in private. Eshun did not reply. The next day the whole community was gathered listening to a teaching by the master. At the end, Eshun stood up and addressed the anonymous writer of the love letter, who was somewhere among the group: "If you love me so much, come and embrace me now!"

This Buddhist nun is beautiful, just like the nun Eshun in the story, but she also looks just as determined not to be distracted from her path to Enlightenment.

The theme of worldly love and sexual desire being hindrances on the spiritual path is a common one. However, this story contains an interesting role reversal, as the majority of these stories have a male protagonist and a female who is in love or in lust with him. Such stories reflect the predominant male view of women as always seeking to turn men's heads from their religious endeavors and entrap them in worldly desires. Such stories imply that women are focused on material concerns, driven by lust and attachment, and therefore unfit to follow a serious religious life or monastic training.

The nun Eshun reverses this stereotype. Despite her great beauty, which would have ensured her a good marriage and wealth, Eshun chose to become a nun and follow an ascetic spiritual life, renouncing all worldly pleasures. It is a monk—a man—who succumbs to her charms, and unable to deal with his desire in an appropriate way, attempts a transgression of the monastic code. Eshun chooses a skillful way to teach him the foolishness of his secret infatuation, one that does not single him out for ridicule or punishment. Though carried out in public, the monk's humiliation was private, and therefore deeply effective. In this way Eshun shows that women can be not only good and dedicated practitioners of Buddha Dharma, but skillful in dealing with problems when they arise.

Naropa's Old Hag

This legend from the biography of Naropa, the eleventh-century Indian Buddhist master, reveals the limitations of an exclusively male, intellectual approach to spiritual practice:

Naropa was a brilliant student, who became abbot of the great Nalanda University and was generally considered the most learned Buddhist monastic of his day. However, although his learning was outstanding, he had not yet reached enlightenment. One day, as he was sitting with his back to the sun, studying texts on logic and epistemology, a terrifying shadow fell upon the page. Looking up, he saw a hideous old woman, who asked him what he was doing. He explained that he was studying Buddhist texts.

Then she asked him, "Which do you understand, the words or the meaning?"

Naropa replied that he understood the meaning.

On hearing this, the hideous old woman started to shake and weep in an awful manner. When Naropa asked why, she told him he was lying, that he understood only the words and not the meaning.

"Who, then, understands the meaning?" demanded Naropa, feeling shocked and desperate because he suddenly acknowledged the truth in her words.

"My brother, Tilopa," she replied.

Naropa then asked her to introduce him to this wonderful teacher, but she told him to seek out Tilopa for himself and disappeared like a rainbow in the sky.

This extract from Naropa's life story is full of symbolism. The terrifying shadow is caused because Naropa has his back to the sun, the light that shines with the clarity of true understanding. The hag who casts the shadow on the page is really Vajrayogini, the female deity who represents the wisdom of *shunyata*, or emptiness. As we learned in Chapter 3, everything that appears to the unenlightened mind seems to exist from its own side. Realizing emptiness allows us to see through this mistaken perception to the true nature of everything that exists. While an intellectual understanding of this view of reality is

A traditional Tibetan Buddhist text, block printed on paper and wrapped in a protective cloth.

A Tibetan Buddhist mother carrying a child on her back.

qualities of intellectual learning with the feminine qualities of meditative wisdom and the realization of emptiness can lead us to awakening. There is however, a human dimension to this story, as Vajrayogini chooses to appear as a hideous old woman to confront the learned monk in his prestigious seat of learning. The unusual event of a woman entering his room would have caused Naropa quite a shock. Thus the underlying message is that true wisdom can be found in unlikely and ordinary people as much as in the learned inhabitants of great monasteries.

Mother's Advice

This story from Japan reinforces the idea that spiritual insight is not limited to the learned and celebrates the Buddhist admiration for a mother's wisdom.

When Jiun, the Shingon Buddhist master, was young, he was fond of delivering lectures to his fellow students that demonstrated his cleverness and knowledge.

When his mother heard about this habit, she wrote Jiun a letter: "Son, I do not think you became a devotee of the Buddha because you desired to turn into a walking dictionary for others. There is no end to information and commentary, glory and honor. I wish you would stop this lecture business. Shut yourself up in a little temple in the remote mountains. Devote yourself to meditation and in this way attain true realization."

necessary, a true realization of emptiness arises only through the practitioner's meditation. As we have also learned, emptiness is linked in the Buddhist tradition with the female principle. Thus the hag, who is actually Vajrayogini, helps Naropa to see that his understanding is limited to the male realm of intellectual knowledge and lacks the dimension of personal experience. Through his encounter with Vajrayogini, Naropa realizes what has been missing from his spiritual endeavors and embarks on an arduous journey to find his teacher, Tilopa, who puts Naropa through the hardest possible tests on his quest for enlightenment.

This tale is concerned with the archetypal feminine principle in Buddhism, rather than a real woman, as the old hag is actually Vajrayogini in disguise. It shows clearly that a dry, academic understanding of Buddhist teachings and principles is insufficient for genuine spiritual progress. Only the harmonious integration of the masculine

Vijaya and Mara

This traditional tale demonstrates that women can resist worldly temptations, personified in Indian mythology as Mara, who could manifest equally as a man or a woman in his attempts to prevent people from awakening.

Vijaya was a beautiful young woman of humble background born during the Buddha's lifetime. Inspired by her wealthy friend Khema, who renounced her privileged life and became ordained, Vijaya also decided to become a nun and follow the Buddha. As gifted and virtuous as she was beautiful, Vijaya was meditating deeply and was close to *reaching enlightenment. Just as Mara had appeared to the Buddha in the form of beautiful young women to attempt to distract him from his meditative concentration, he appeared to Vijaya as a handsome young man and attempted to seduce her. However, Vijaya was unmoved. She replied thus to his seductive entreaties: "I delight in observing emptiness, the unreality of the body, and don't desire your soft touches. My ignorance is dispelled." Realizing that he had no power to change Vijaya's mind, Mara slunk off defeated.*

This picture of the Buddha's enlightenment shows Mara's daughters trying, but failing, to seduce the Buddha. Mara is shown on the left, with bow and arrow.

As this story demonstrates, despite being often thought of by men as weak-willed and desirous of sensual pleasures, women and nuns were as capable of resisting seduction by Mara as was the Buddha. Though tales with this theme are not commonplace and must be seen alongside many stories showing women to be inferior to men and often trying to seduce them, nonetheless, this story is a powerful affirmation for women. Vijaya's example shows a woman not only attaining enlightenment but successfully resisting the charms of Mara. Buddha overcame Mara first and set an example that other women and men could follow. Vijaya's story carries the message that, ultimately, gender doesn't matter. As did the Buddha before her, she simply carries on with her meditation despite temptation until she realizes her goal of enlightenment.

A group of Tibetan Buddhist pilgrims looking at the Himalayan mountains in western Tibet. The mountains draw pilgrims from around the globe.

Three Contemporary Buddhist Women Teachers

So when I had my first child, people expected me to stop teaching,
and when expecting my second, they said, "Now surely she will stop teaching";
but I did not. Having children did not mean the conclusion of being a
meditator and a teacher.

—CHRISTINA FELDMAN, CONTEMPORARY BUDDHIST TEACHER, QUOTED IN MARTINE BACHELOR,

WALKING ON LOTUS FLOWERS

We turn now to the lives and ideas of three modern Buddhist female teachers. As we see, their experiences celebrate the capacity of women to strive as practitioners and teachers for the goal of enlightenment.

Sharon Salzberg

Sharon has been a student of Buddhism since 1970 and has been leading meditation retreats worldwide since 1974. She teaches both intensive awareness practice (vipassana or insight meditation) and the profound cultivation of lovingkindness and compassion (the *Brahma Viharas*). She is cofounder of the Insight Meditation Society in Barre, Massachusetts, The Barre Center for Buddhist Studies, and The Forest Refuge, a new center for long-term meditation practice. She is author of several audio tapes and books on Buddhism, including *A Heart as Wide as the World: Stories on the Path of Lovingkindness*, and is coauthor (with Joseph Goldstein) of a correspondence course on Insight Meditation.

Q: *Asian Buddhist teachers are mainly men and monastic. How did this fact affect you when you began teaching? Has this balance changed much over the years?*

A: None of my early teachers were monastic. S. N. Goenka, who led my first retreat in India, was a businessman with five children. Munindra was a semi-monastic, an *anagarika*, living with more precepts than a lay person but far less than a monk. He didn't wear the formal robes or adhere to the rules of any order. And my teacher Dipa-Ma was a woman—a widow and a mother. It wasn't until I practiced with Sayadaw U Pandita in Burma in 1984 that I had a teacher who was a monastic. Because my teachers were primarily lay people, I always had the sense that one could lead a lay life and have strong realizations, if one's motivation was strong enough.

Has the situation changed much over the years? In terms of Asia, I don't know. But certainly, in the West there are many lay teachers and many women teachers.

Q: *What do you feel is the most important message in Buddhism for Western people to focus on?*

A: I think the most important message in Buddhism for Western people is Right Effort, because it's a very tricky one for Westerners to understand. There's so much emphasis placed on Right Effort in classical Buddhist teachings, and it's meant to be empowering: No one can give you the truth, but also no one can take it away from you. The very teaching of Right Effort implies a capacity within us to be free. It's a capacity inherent in everyone, not just in a few select, special people. We simply need to make the effort to bring it to flower.

That's what I think the meaning of Right Effort really is. Yet we don't trust that inner capacity, so when we hear a message about effort, it points to our insufficiencies rather than to our innate potential. Then, too, we don't know *how* to make the effort. We try too hard, or we castigate ourselves the whole time we're trying.

When Sayadaw U Pandita came to Barre in 1984, it was his first trip to the West, and some of the people sitting with him had never been to Asia and were not used to that idiom of teaching. At the end of an interview, he would often say, "Try harder." That was his way of saying goodbye. It wasn't meant to imply that you weren't trying hard enough or that you weren't a good person. It was just a reminder of the power of Right Effort. But people would be upset when he said it.

The difficulties people have with the concept of effort and with respecting their own capacity for enlightenment get translated into a kind of doubt. Very few people say, "Well, I don't really believe I can do it." They're more likely to say, "It's not worth doing." Right Effort really means not holding back, being full-hearted in what we do, with the confidence that we have the

ability to see the truth for ourselves. If we could understand that, I think it would be a great blessing for the West.

Q: *How have your teaching experiences affected your understanding of Buddhism? And has your teaching experience changed your own practice?*
A: My teaching experiences have given me access to the process of unfolding in other people, not just in myself. Seeing the same truths displayed over and over again has reinforced my appreciation for the teachings of Buddhism: Attachment causes suffering. How ungovernable the conditions of our lives are. How we need to find a quality of happiness that differs from conventional happiness, which will shatter and break as conditions change.

Teaching has changed my own practice in that it reminds me of the timelessness of the journey and how being impatient doesn't serve us. We need to take one step at a time. The mystery of how things unfold has been reinforced by my teaching experience: Watching people struggle; then seeing their awareness break open. And it breaks open not

because they tried harder but because they relaxed. Or seeing that what seemed to be a very difficult period was, in retrospect, very fruitful. The vantage point of a teacher is a different kind of perspective.

Q: *As Buddhism comes west it needs to adapt partially to a different culture. How different do you feel your teaching is, in both style and content, from that of an indigenous Buddhist teacher?*
A: I hesitate to make such a clear division between the East and the West, because one hopes that essentially it's the same teaching. Regarding the teacher-student relationship, the Buddha himself talked about the teacher as a spiritual friend. That's what it's meant to be. In Asia, there's a whole spectrum of ways teachers relate to their students. Some are very authoritative and demanding, and some are buddies and supportive. If their motivation is pure, they're not interested in their own aggrandizement; they're interested in the well-being of the student. It's just a stylistic difference. To label all Asian teachers "authoritarian" and all Western teachers "free spirits" doesn't seem right.

That said, we in the West tend to feel freer to question authority and that invigorates the teachings in a lot of ways. It can be a problem for students if they question the practice so much that they never try it. But the questioning also infuses energy into a teaching, so that students do not accept it on blind faith and do something just because a respected elder has said so, but because they want to see it for themselves. I think that's positive.

Q: *What is your experience of being a Buddhist woman? Do you think it might be very different from a male experience?*
A: It hasn't been different for me, because I've never felt discriminated against in my access to great teachers or in my ability to have teachings. I've never felt disrespect from the male hierarchy in my role as a teacher. But part of that is because I'm a lay woman. If I were to become a nun and join the Buddhist hierarchy, it would be a very different experience.

In Asia, depending on the setting, it would probably be very different. In some places, there are situations for nuns that are quite good in allowing practice, study, discipline. There are other places where nuns are mostly cooking and cleaning for the monks.

Q: *What advice would you offer to people beginning the Buddhist path?*
A: Persevere. Everything's in the practice. Maybe the best advice I ever got was from my teacher Munindra, with whom I studied while I was living in India, not on intensive retreat. I was having great difficulty maintaining a daily practice, because when things felt good in my sitting, I'd be delirious with happiness and think, "Oh, great, I'm going to stay here forever." And then when things felt painful or difficult, I would be very discouraged and just give up, thinking "I can't do this" or "It's not right." I went up and down, all the time. Finally I went to him with my problem.

Munindra said, "I have one piece of advice for you: Put your body there. Every day, just put your body there. Sometimes your sitting will feel one way, and sometimes it will feel another way. The most important thing is that you do it."

To support that, it's wonderful to have a teacher. But if you're in a situation where you can't have a teacher, then it's good to have some kind of community, a sangha, to help you "put your body there."

Q: *How do you see Buddhism affecting Western culture, and vice versa? Is there a danger of the essence of Buddhism becoming diluted in the West?*
A: I think what's going to happen to Buddhism in the West is the whole spectrum of manifestation. Some of it will be diluted. We see that already in ads showing monks buying computers and Buddha images with jewelry draped over them. That's one level.

Then there's the level of partial interest. Some people will take the parts of the Buddha's teaching that appeal to them and leave aside whole tracks. There will be people interested in the philosophy without the practice, and people interested in the practice without the philosophy. Some people will be interested in both.

I don't fear that Buddhism will be undone by the West, that it will be so terribly corrupted that it will be unrecognizable. I think there will always be people who embrace the ethical basis of Buddhist teaching and people who do the practice and attain liberation.

I think Buddhism's greatest effect on Western culture is going to be in the introduction of the practices. Even people who are devout Christians or Jews seem to take an interest in the meditation practices of Buddhism. Some have said that their practice of Buddhist meditation has reinvigorated their appreciation of their own faith and their ability to practice it more mindfully. Practitioners

become more aware of their own experience: the state of their minds and their level of focus, whole-heartedness, and compassion.

I think that another way Western culture will affect Buddhism is by introducing a note of non-sectarianism. In Asia, different Buddhist schools have existed without much dialogue for a very long time. In the West, they're all running into each other. The mode of being in the West is more about dialogue and discussion, and that's going to influence how the different Buddhist schools regard themselves and each other. And because Asian monasticism hasn't taken root here as strongly as lay practice has, it will be interesting to see what happens to the monastic tradition and to Buddhism in general, with a largely lay sangha.

One difference between East and West is that different kinds of faith tend to predominate in each culture, and we probably need to balance them. In Buddhism, the first stage of faith is "bright faith," which means falling in love with the teachings and the possibility of your own freedom. It's a very exciting, open state. The next stage is "verified faith," which is based on your own experience. It comes through your questioning and wondering and practicing, not on being with a teacher or in a sacred place. In the West, we tend to be better at verified faith than bright faith, whereas in Asian society, the questioning is likely to be more muted than the devotion. We need both kinds of faith, so questioning is something Westerners are bringing to Asian practitioners, and devotion is something Asian practitioners are bringing to the West.

Martine Batchelor

Martine grew up in France, and after traveling extensively in her youth, ended up in Korea. After a visit of a few days to the Songgwangsa Monastery in South Korea, she became a Korean Zen nun at the monastery and lived there for ten years. When her teacher, Ven. Kusan Sunim, died, she returned to the West, married, and moved to Sharpham, then a Buddhist community in Devon. Currently, she is a Guiding Teacher at Gaia House Meditation Retreat Centre and a Founding Teacher of Sharpham College of Buddhist Studies and Contemporary Inquiry. Martine gives talks, leads retreats, and participates in conferences worldwide. She is the author of several books on Buddhism and meditation, including *Walking on Lotus Flowers: Women Living, Loving, and Meditating* and *Meditation for Life.*

Q: *What were your first experiences of teaching and leading retreats?*
A: Wonderful, inspiring.

Q: *During these early experiences, did you ever feel that being a woman was especially helpful or a hindrance in any way?*
A: It was good to teach as a couple, together with my husband, Stephen. Being complementary, according to the retreatants' needs or tendencies, we could both be of benefit to them in different ways.

Q: *As a renowned Buddhist teacher, you are asked to teach and lead retreats internationally, but mostly in Western countries where female spiritual authority figures are easily accepted. Do you have experiences of teaching in traditional Asian Buddhist countries, and is there any difference?*
A: I have taught in Thailand but in centers where women are highly regarded, so there were no differences.

Q: *You teach/lead retreats with both female only and mixed male and female participants. What are*

A Buddhist temple, glimpsed through the trees at the entrance. Inside the temple complex is a meditation hall, where monks and nuns meditate.

the differences, if any? Women-only groups may make women feel more supported or safe in some way, but can this also be counterproductive?

A: I rarely teach women-only groups. I have participated in female-only groups and days of meditation, and it is an interesting feeling, especially when the women are very engaged in the practice and the spiritual life. There is generally a great warmth, openness, support, and a special way of listening. It can only be counterproductive if the time is used to complain about men!

Q: *You teach both on your own and with your husband. Do you ever experience participants looking more to him for answers/spiritual authority? If so, is this undermining for you in any way?*

A: Stephen and I are quite different. I am more practical, down-to-earth, and experiential, and he is more scholastic, existential, and philosophical. So according to their own inclinations or needs at any given time, people might go more to me or to Stephen.

Q: *You were a nun for ten years, and now teach as a lay Buddhist. Do you perceive different responses from those you teach as a lay person from when you wore robes? Do you notice Western students react differently to monastic Buddhist and lay Buddhist teachers?*

A: I never taught Westerners in the West as a nun. Western students generally react according to their own inclinations. If they are very Buddhist and pious, they behave very reverentially to a monastic, as I would myself, anyway. It is just Buddhistic

conditioning and respect for the robes. However, if they are antireligious or skeptical or a beginner, they often feel uncomfortable and do not behave especially respectfully toward a monastic teacher. Then often they feel more comfortable toward me as a lay woman and can talk to me more easily and with respect. Personally, I try to make people relax and laugh if possible and try not to encourage too much piety, unless it is in the temperament of the person. Then I accept it supportively.

Q: *Being a female Buddhist teacher must be both deeply rewarding and carry a great deal of responsibility. Could you tell us something about your feelings on this?*

A: Being a teacher, female or male, is a responsibility no matter the gender: We all must be true to the tradition, be mindful not to mislead people, try to understand them and not cause them any harm, and be tolerant and open to where they are coming from. When I am being a teacher, I treat them all with respect and kindness; I am always ready to listen.

Q: *Does your role as a teacher strengthen and reinforce your own Buddhist practice? Do you feel you need more time for your own practice after the demands of teaching or leading a retreat?*

A: Teaching is very inspiring and challenging. It helps me to inquire, to reflect, and to ponder. Leading a retreat is real Buddhist practice for me, since I do all the sittings with the participants and try to practice even more what I am teaching. I also learn from the participants; they show me angles I had not thought of. I find teaching retreats great practice time.

Ven. Ani Tenzin Palmo

Here, in her own words, are the experiences of Ani Tenzin Palmo, a British woman who became a Tibetan Buddhist nun. She spent twelve years meditating in a cave, as recounted in the book *Cave in the Snow*, and now teaches around the world:

Born during the Second World War, I was brought up in London and came across the dharma in my teens during the early sixties. Discovering a connection with Tibetan Buddhism, which was at that time almost unknown in the West, I left for India at the age of twenty to work at a small school in Dalhousie for incarnate lamas, which was run by a lady named Freda Bedi. There, on my twenty-first birthday, I met His Excellency Khamtrul Rinpoche and, three weeks later, received my first ordination as a nun.

Khamtrul Rinpoche is the head of a Tibetan community comprising 130 monks and about 400 lay people. I worked as Khamtrul Rinpoche's secretary and taught English to the young monks. After some years, the community moved to their present location, known as Tashi Jong, and then Rinpoche told me to go to the Himalayan Valley of Lahaul in order to undertake retreats and deepen the practice. So, I went to live in the small monastery of Tayul Gonpa. Lahaul lies at about eleven thousand feet and is usually cut off from the rest of India by snow for about six to eight months of the year.

I stayed in Tayul Gonpa for about six years but then felt the need for further isolation and moved into a cave about an hour away from the monastery. There I lived for twelve years, although usually I went to Tashi Jong once a year to visit

Khamtrul Rinpoche. The last three years, I stayed in solitary retreat.

In 1988, I left India and went to stay with friends in the hills outside of the medieval town of Assisi in Italy. However, after some years, I returned to India in order to start teaching English to the young incarnation of Khamtrul Rinpoche, who was then twelve years old. Around this time, some of the other Rinpoches of the Khampagar monastery requested me to start a nunnery, as there was nothing for nuns at our community.

Living in Lahaul, it was easy to see that while the monks were out front performing the *pujas* [offering ceremonies], receiving teachings, and undertaking long retreats, the nuns were usually in the kitchen doing the cooking and so forth. So many of the nuns were intelligent and devoted, but there was no opportunity for them to receive education or practice the more profound teachings.

Obviously, it is not much use simply to bemoan the fact without doing something to improve the situation. So when the lamas requested me to start a nunnery, I recalled that on a few occasions His Excellency the Eighth Khamtrul Rinpoche had suggested organizing a nunnery, but at that period, I had to put this dream aside. Now was the time, so I went to Asia to try to raise some awareness of our nunnery project. This was not easy, as I had no contacts and am not a high lama sitting on a throne, wearing a brocade hat. However, slowly people began to take an interest. Many people remarked that in all the years of donating for monasteries and monks, I was the first person talking about *nuns!*

About this time, Vicki Mackenzie asked me to allow her to write the story of my life and especially about the years that I spent in the cave. This was subsequently published as *Cave in the Snow*, a book in which Vicki managed to turn an obscure account of staying in retreat into a fascinating page-turner that has inspired so many people from many different backgrounds! This book also helped toward making the plight of nuns more widely appreciated.

Our nunnery is designed for girls from the Himalayan regions, such as Tibet, Ladakh, Nepal, Kinnaur, Spiti, and so forth. Traditionally nuns in these areas received little opportunity to study,

although in Tibet itself, nuns often became good practitioners. In the border regions, the nuns were little better than unpaid servants for their families or the monasteries. They were devout but uneducated and often prayed that in their next lives, they might be reborn with a male body in order to have the advantages needed to accomplish the dharma path. In the past it was often difficult for women to gain access to the teaching or the teachers, but this situation is gradually changing all over the Buddhist world, as the needs of the female half of the human race are slowly being acknowledged.

However, in the West and in modern Asia, this problem is much less serious. Women are highly educated and articulate. They can read whatever they wish and attend whatever teachings are being offered. There is no restriction as to gender. Our essential Buddha Nature—the unborn naked awareness—is neither male nor female. All unenlightened beings are tormented by the basic five poisons of deluded ignorance, greed, anger, envy, and pride. If women have difficulties, men also have their own problems. That is the unsatisfactory nature of samsara. If not one thing, then it is another. But that is how we learn and grow.

It is said that women are often more openly emotional than men. Their moods often swing up and down, and they respond to events through feelings rather than with rational thought. Whether or not this is a broad stereotype based on a male perception, the positive side is that when these feelings are brought under some control (instead of being the controller), this releases a great energy that propels the female practitioner faster and higher than her more cautious and pedantic male counterpart. A number of Asian meditation teachers have remarked to me that women take to meditation easily and are not intimidated by the wordless, intuitive qualities of the meditative mind. They feel at home in the Unknown.

Buddhism is a path that encompasses the body, speech, and mind. The fundamental tenets of the dharma are as relevant and authentic today as they were twenty-five hundred years ago. The basic viewpoint transcends social customs and beliefs and speaks straight to the heart of anyone who is open. It is not a matter of dogma and beliefs. It is a wonderful relief to hear such profound sense as well as that dharma, which goes beyond our everyday logic into a world of experience both paradoxical and truly sane.

In our hectic and over-stressed lives, with their emphasis on material success and physical rewards, there is a growing sense of inner hollowness and futility. Thinking people are becoming increasingly conscious of a deep hunger for something that will give true satisfaction in their lives. So there is a genuine search for meaning beneath the outer exotic or esoteric layers that the dharma sometimes presents. We want to know how to be happy, peaceful, kind, and understanding. We need to know how to cope skillfully with our families, relationships, professions, and social lives.

Traditionally, the Buddha Dharma was mainly in the hands of the "professionals"—the sangha or community of ordained monks and nuns. These were people who had gone forth in faith from the household life of family and profession to devote themselves to the study, practice, and teaching of the dharma. In this way, the dharma has been passed down through the ages up to the present time. The role of lay people in general was to lead good and kind lives in accordance with the precepts and to support the sangha in their lives of immersion in the dharma. Of course, there have always been some lay scholars and practitioners, especially in certain traditions, but the monastic sangha is still viewed as the repository and preserver of the doctrine.

Nowadays, as the dharma spreads in the West, it is mainly practiced and studied by those who are lay people, not the ordained sangha. Naturally, this change is likely to have an impact on how the dharma is perceived and passed on. Areas that have deep import to renunciants will have much less appeal to those within relationships or with family ties. I notice myself that, when speaking with other monks and nuns, I can express views that I would not speak of to the non-ordained for fear of hurting their feelings. Thus the emphasis of the dharma will undergo a shift.

Most people who come to the dharma in the West or in modern Asia do not have the space or the time for much formal practice. A ten-day meditation course is the most that the majority can aspire to. People sometimes ask me if years-long meditation retreats are really necessary for enlightenment, and I do not know how to answer in a way that will not make them feel despairing or resentful of their present lives and relationships. Even as I type this, I am of two minds.

The fact is that the Lord Buddha himself found it necessary to leave his palace, wife, and newborn son.

After his enlightenment, he did not return to the lay life but encouraged others also to renounce the world. The great practitioners of the past usually spent years in retreat. Some spent their whole lives in strict practice. Their lives were dedicated to realizing the dharma. Even the lay practitioners usually spent many years of meditation in hermitages and caves before marrying. In marriage, they dedicated themselves to the dharma by becoming scholars, traditional doctors, or household yogis [ngags.pa]. They lived in a society that was much more leisured and nondistracted. They did not need to go off to the office or factory every day, surrounded by colleagues with a very different world view and interests. Long retreats allow for the inner world to unfold and our minds to blend completely with the practice. The great masters do not *practice* the dharma, they *are* the dharma.

So, we need to tailor the dharma to our needs and situations. Since the majority of people who come to Buddhism nowadays are not prepared to renounce their present lifestyles, we must use the practices in a skillful manner that can be integrated into our hearts and lives. Personally, I feel that in our overcomplicated and stressful modern world, the need is for simplicity, rather than elaborate visualizations and complex philosophical sophistry. Those approaches were valid for a culture that was quite simple (for instance, in traditional societies, there was no television, radio, newspapers, magazines, or novels), but our modern minds are not empty canvases on which to inscribe elaborate designs. Our minds are already overstuffed with garbage and need to be cleared out to allow some inner space.

The Himalayan mountain range. Tenzin Palmo's years of retreat would have given her a similar view.

Therefore, I advise people to practice the basic principles, such as the Six Perfections or *paramitas*, which include qualities such as generosity, ethics, patience, and effort that we can all incorporate into our everyday lives, as well as meditation and wisdom that we cultivate in order to transform our ordinary lives into on-going dharma practice. Mindfulness or present awareness is beneficial at all times, of course, and where better to practice lovingkindness and compassion than with our family and colleagues?

The West also seems inclined to use meditation as a kind of psychotherapy to make us feel better.

A group of young Tibetan Buddhist nuns studying. Tenzin Palmo has founded a nunnery in northern India to give more nuns from the Himalayan regions the opportunity to devote their lives to Buddhist practice.

Yet, meditation should enable us to see directly all thoughts and feelings as empty and the subject or viewer as empty also. Our memories and hang-ups, traumas and inhibitions, are empty. They are not me or mine. The experience of the nature of the mind, the naked unborn awareness, goes far beyond any of these ego-bound psychological preoccupations. Meditation is not just to make us feel nice or solve our emotional problems.

Meditation is to overcome and annihilate directly the very basis of all our problems: belief in and clinging to an ego and to the subject/object conceptual thinking that results from that false view. Everything follows from that.

To follow through safely on any unknown path, it is advisable to have a reliable guide. Even the best guidebook or map will not include every by-path, detour, or obstacle, and it is easy to go astray, even with the best intentions. A guide must, of course, be someone who knows the whole route—by experience and not just by hearsay. He or she must be trustworthy and able to give directions and cautions suitable to the individual traveler. Likewise on the spiritual path, one looks for a teacher who *knows* the way through direct realization as well as through study and through having themselves practiced under learned masters. The teacher must understand the pupils better than they understand themselves. It is not enough to be charismatic or witty. It is not enough to be famous and to have a large following. Sometimes the greatest masters are quite ordinary on the outside and live hidden lives, eschewing fame or many students.

In this modern world it is very difficult to judge who is and who is not a genuine master able to lead others successfully on the spiritual path. What is the atmosphere like around the teacher, and how do the students relate with each other? Look at the main disciples after twenty years with the teacher. See what has become of them. Do they embody qualities that are truly admirable—not just more intellectual knowledge? Are they kinder, more compassionate, more harmonious, peaceful, and wise than the average person? Or, at least, more so than when they began? Is this how one would like to become? Find out what is the general reputation of this teacher outside of his/her own circle of admirers. We should not be naive in entrusting our minds to another.

Also, just because a teacher is suitable for one person does not necessarily make him/her suitable for another. This is a very individual matter and depends on infinite causes. The heart usually knows intuitively, but the intellect can also do some checking up. The heart guru is the one who points out the nature of our unborn primordial awareness. The heart guru is inseparable from the *dharmakaya* [enlightened] nature of our mind because he or she *is* the dharmakaya embodied. To meet such a teacher requires prior karmic connections and prayers of aspiration. However, we still have to walk the path with our own feet.

Meantime, the dharma exists and is still able to be realized. There are many excellent books available and many centers and teachers. We can learn so much from so many without the need for a lifetimes-long commitment to the first teacher we come across. Regard all teachers as spiritual friends who come in many guises—not always seated on high brocade thrones! We certainly should not postpone our entry into and practice of the dharma until we meet the "perfect Master." With our present unruly and uncultivated minds, even meeting the Buddha himself would not help much. First, we must prepare our minds to receive the blessings and realizations on the path; then the right teachers will appear as the need arises.

CHAPTER FIVE
THE FEMININE FACE OF BUDDHIST ART

*Many of my early paintings are
expressionist and full of suffering… Now
I try to paint naturally. You can radiate
the natural state everywhere. You can even
emanate kindness in paintings.*

—YAHNE LE TOUMELIN

The Origins of Buddhist Figurative Art

From the beginning Buddhism has always regarded wisdom (prajna) as feminine,
just as the Greeks regarded Sophia as the goddess of wisdom.
Throughout the millennia countless scholars, artists, and poets
have extolled the immaculate beauty of her form.
She is sister, mother, lover, and child—the divine muse
who conceives everything that is imaginable and brings it all into existence.

—ROBERT BEER, *PEACEFUL DEITIES IN VAJRAYANA BUDDHISM*

As Stephen Batchelor points out, for the first five hundred years after he achieved enlightenment, the Buddha "was not represented as a human being. In the carved rock reliefs and sculptures that survive, he was suggested only through symbols—an eight-spoked wheel, an empty throne, a tree, a pair of footprints." (*The Awakening of the West*) Only after Alexander had conquered much of Asia and the Greek King Menander ruled in India and converted to Buddhism did figurative representations of the Buddha in human form begin to be made. Because the Buddha had transcended human limitations, it had not occurred to his followers to represent him in human form. They believed that the Buddha had departed this world and entered nirvana, and that human images can tell us nothing about this enlightened state. However, part of the assimilation of the Greeks into Indian culture included representing the Buddha in the usual ways of the Hellenic tradition. The Greeks had an extensive pantheon of gods in idealized human form, and from these heroic figures arose the first images of the Buddha.

The oldest Buddhist tradition, Theravada Buddhism, which has its origins in the years immediately following the Buddha's life, has relatively few iconographical figures. The early Indian sculptures that do exist are mostly of the Buddha himself, together with early forms of the major bodhisattvas. When Buddhism spread beyond India into Southeast Asia, these images were influenced by local culture. Thus there are Thai, Burmese, and Sri Lankan images of the Buddha alongside the earliest Indian images, each influenced by the artistic tradition of those countries. In addition to these images,

A non-figurative image of the Buddha, this eight-spoked wheel represents the turning of the wheel of Dharma and the Noble Eightfold Path.

An early Gandhara standing bodhisattva from western India. Although Buddhist, it incorporates strong classical Greek influences from the time of Alexander the Great.

practices within the Theravada tradition, and Kuan Yin is associated more closely with the Mahayana and Zen traditions, Ajahn Yai Guong Saeng established these temples as oases of female sacredness in a country almost devoid of the feminine aspect of Buddhism. The main temple is run by women, who manage temple affairs and also sculpt statues and paint murals and pictures of Kuan Yin. A woman visitor to this temple described her experience there as follows: "I feel joy when I am here at Kwan Yin Temple. The smell of incense floats on the breeze. The tree leaves move gently. A mantra resounds in homage to Kwan Yin and blesses the temple, surrounding neighborhood, and all beings near or far. Female images abide in all directions. There is something that I can connect with here as a woman." (Catherine Altman, in *Seeds of Peace*, Vol. 17, No. 2.)

Theravada and early Buddhist art includes depictions of empty spaces, such as images of the Buddha's footprints or an empty throne. These symbolize that the Buddha has departed this world for nirvana. There are few Theravadan icons of female figures, either from the early years of Buddhism or from the later artistic traditions of the countries where Theravada Buddhism developed.

An interesting exception are the images that fill two modern temples dedicated to Kuan Yin in Thailand, created by Ven. Ajahn Yai Guong Saeng, a great female Buddhist teacher. Although she

Like the story of Chatsumarn told in Chapter 2, the establishment of such women-centered places demonstrates a positive change toward the feminine in Buddhism in Thailand. As the world becomes smaller through the ease of international travel, Buddhism has moved west, and the modern consciousness of honoring the feminine within Buddhism, and in society at large, has moved east. As we in the West have benefited so profoundly from the Buddha's teachings, it is only fitting that we offer something back which helps to create a more harmonious balance between male and female in traditional Buddhist countries.

The importance of balancing male images of the Buddha with representations of the feminine face of Buddhism is made explicit in the art of a modern Western Buddhist woman, as we read in the story below.

Mary Reinard

Mary is an American practitioner of Theravada Buddhism and an artist who is exploring iconographical forms, including female Buddha figures:

As the baby girl of four sisters and four brothers, space was an unaffordable luxury. It was 1958, and our two-story bungalow had double beds in each of four bedrooms. I was fortunate to have a sleeping area all to myself, though my four-year-old body more than filled the tiny crib. One September afternoon, I noticed that someone had mistakenly wandered into my territory. As I peered between the bars of my tiny crib, I saw a wee baby swimming in oceans of soft golden sheets. Not till night drew near did I realize my sanctuary would never be returned to its rightful owner. Lights out. I was lifted into a big double bed and began to let down my defenses. This new bed was huge and could surely offer a refuge from my rambunctious surroundings. Quickly falling asleep, I awoke hours later to find myself crammed between two of my teenaged siblings. My refuge was truly gone: I would begin to search for another. It didn't take long.

Christmas Eve arrived. The door opened to a number of firemen holding boxes and offering huge smiles. Except for the little red tricycle with a bow on the handle, none of us exceedingly animated children could tell what was hidden beneath the tantalizing wrappings. When Dad finally arrived home from work, he took on a near-hero persona as he cheerfully suggested we each pick out one present that night, saving the rest for Christmas morning. I opened a big box of chalk.

I have been an artist since I can recall. I've drawn from within on a feeling of spacious calm ever since I opened that first box of chalk, nearly forty-three years ago. Yet as an adult, I would still struggle to integrate my internal refuge with the external world. I shared with a trusted friend this hope for integration. Charles asked me to describe the process I experienced while painting. What did I notice when preparing to draw?

"Well," I began, concerned he wouldn't understand, "It's like this ... I paint from a place of joy. In order to feel this joy I need to get emotionally balanced with the world. So, I start by focusing on my feelings. What emotion arises as dominant? Once this is clear, I invite this feeling tone to be held in my heart, and my mind begins to settle. When my mind is settled, then I can see how various parts of my body are responding to this dominant emotion. Then I invite the body to relax around this feeling. If I notice strong emotional discomfort, I simply wait till it passes before moving on. If I can't get past discomfort, then everything is colored by this uneasiness, it's impossible to relax the body, and I'll never find the balance that I'm searching for. By *balance*, I mean a feeling of stability. If I really concentrate, I can always find a place of stable balance. Painting helps to maintain this balance.

When balance is maintained, then a joy arises that I can't seem to access in any other way. That's when I begin to draw, that's why I paint. This joy is my refuge."

Charles grinned like the Cheshire Cat: "Sounds just like meditation." From his bookshelves, he handed me *Buddha's Little Instruction Book* by Jack Kornfield. I've been meditating ever since.

Nine months later: First retreat, second day, just beginning the evening period. My legs and mind were screaming. Silently admitting defeat, I decided to exit the property quietly first thing in the morning. Relief was followed by a huge weight of tension lifting from my body. Released tension relaxed the mind, and for the first time during the retreat, the imminent threat of anguish subsided. I was no longer fearful that I would lose control and go screaming out of the room. Without this narrative of fear lording over my experience, there was space to review options: How best might I endure the rest of the retreat? Again I noticed the mind relax, but this time my body registered a familiar feeling. The word *paint* came to mind. Having no tools present other than body and mind, it dawned on me that I could still paint, only this time there would be no finished piece. Painting and meditation settled into balance, and to my surprise, a very familiar joy began to rise. A search for the roots of "Buddha's instructions" commenced.

In the spring of the following year, I was met with a familiar sight. Only this time, the stranger draped in golden sheets was a full-grown man: Ajahn Amaro, a Theravadan monk, who was coleading a retreat. Struck by his calm demeanor and gleefully piercing eyes, I determined to find out the source of his teachings. I soon came upon it: third shelf from the bottom and halfway down the stack. I read every book I could find by Ajahn Sumedho and then those by his teacher Achaan Chah. Heck, I thought I might as well get to know the whole family!

Virginia, a devout Catholic and Christian iconographer, is both my art teacher and Ajahn Sumedho's sister. Her house is full of beautiful icons. I inquired why she did iconography. She replied, "Producing an icon is a form of meditative prayer. The purpose of this vocation is to bring familiar form to the divine." In accepting me as her student, she strongly suggested: "You create icons that represent where you connect spiritually; stay within your spiritual roots." I paint Buddhist icons.

Ten layers of ground-chalk gesso cover an 8 x 10-inch wooden board. The familiar form of a woman is sketched out in India ink. She rests in enlightened pose on a blossomed white lotus. Holding an egg-shaped stone, I polish the gold leaf that surrounds her. Several hours pass, and the muscles in the palm of my hand began to throb. I loosen my grip. Swinging the arm back and forth repeatedly tires it, and the word *meditate* comes to mind. But out of this repetitive, uncomfortable, and mundane act, a smooth, golden surface begins to emerge. Delight arises. Words spoken over twenty-five hundred years ago by a man donning golden sheets scroll across my mind: "Be a refuge unto yourselves; do not cling to anything else. Take the Dhamma as your refuge; take nothing else as your refuge."

Zen Art

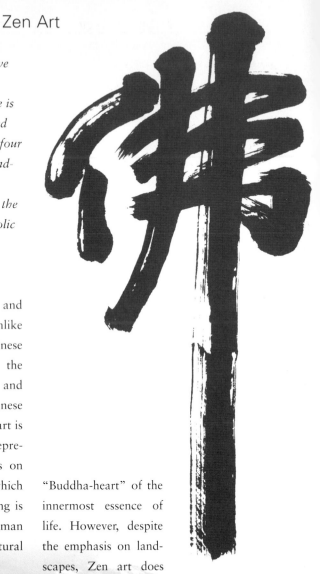

*The particular sect of Buddhism which we
call Zen is precisely the one that is least
involved with pictorial imagery. Yet there is
hardly a stroke ... that is not impregnated
with Zen connotations. The cycle of the four
seasons, the rocks and the pines in ... land-
scapes, the herons, the plum branch, the
very emptiness of white ground between the
strokes of ... ink, all this has deep symbolic
and philosophical significance.*

—ELISE GRILLI, *SESSHU*

Zen Buddhism came to Japan from China and
permeated the entire culture. However, unlike
China, where Ch'an—the original form of Chinese
Zen—was almost entirely wiped out by the
Communist revolution of the last century, Zen and
its influence still remain in contemporary Japanese
life. As Elise Grilli indicates above, much Zen art is
concerned with nature rather than with the representation of Buddhist figures. This emphasis on
nature derives from Chinese ink painting, which
was inextricably linked with Zen. Zen painting is
beyond the dualities of male and female, human
and nature; it attempts to understand the natural
universe and humankind's place within it.

Zen artists, such as the great fifteenth-century
Japanese painter Sesshu, tried to capture in their
work illuminating flashes that revealed the underlying unity of all phenomena. Landscape painting
was regarded as being closest to the totality of
nature and was thought to encompass the
"Buddha-heart" of the
innermost essence of
life. However, despite
the emphasis on land-
scapes, Zen art does
include some figure paintings, as well as pictures
that symbolize or illustrate the attainment of
enlightenment. Among the figures represented in
such works are the great patriarchs of Zen, who
were all male, as well as various gods and deities,
including the great female bodhisattva Kuan Yin.

Artistic Representations of Kuan Yin

Art has been one of the most powerful and effective media through which the Chinese people have come to know Kuan-Yin. It is also through art that one can most clearly detect the bodhisattva's gradual, yet undeniable sexual transformation.

—CHUN-FANG YU, *KUAN-YIN: THE CHINESE TRANSFORMATION OF AVALOKITESHVARA*

As we saw in Chapter 3, scholars do not agree on a single reason why Kuan Yin transformed from male to female, though several sometimes conflicting hypotheses have been put forward. As Chun-Fang Yu informs us, one of these theories is

This lovely painting shows a variation of Kuan Yin of the South Sea. The graceful figure of the bodhisattva is seated by the sea, with the vase of willow branches close by.

that the bodhisattva actually became female through figurative representations of her in paintings, embroidered pictures, and sculptures.

The transformation of the bodhisattva from male to female gave women a positive role model. However, the increasingly female forms of Kuan Yin did not empower Chinese women generally, as there were no significant improvements in women's social status in China during the time of the flowering of the female forms of the bodhisattva. Women were still regarded as "polluting" in the Chinese cultural understanding of the day. However, as a bodhisattva and a goddess, Kuan Yin was a symbol of purity transcending the everyday realities of menstruation, sexual intercourse, and childbirth. Thus, her various female forms symbolized an idealized vision of femininity.

Art historians have identified thirty-three forms of Kuan Yin in Sino-Japanese art, though fourteen of these are simply descriptive. Thus the differences between them are not always apparent, and some forms can be known by more than one name. The most popular of these forms, White Robed Kuan Yin, was the first of the female forms of the bodhisattva to manifest. As noted in Chapter 3, White Robed Kuan Yin is similar in appearance to the male Water Moon Kuan Yin from which she developed, but there are crucial differences: Details on the face have changed; there is no moustache; and the features are drawn with fine lines suggesting femininity, beauty, and grace. The bodhisattva's body has also become more supple and is depicted with the graceful sway of a woman's form.

Another of the female forms of the bodhisattva is known as Kuan Yin with the Fish Basket. She holds a fish basket in her left hand. Fish Basket Kuan Yin is a popular painted image in China, and there is a temple dedicated to her in Mita, Tokyo, Japan, called Gyoran Kannon Temple. Fish Basket Kuan Yin is sometimes confusingly known as Mr. Ma's Wife, although the two figures have quite different iconography. Rather than a fish basket, Mr. Ma's Wife is sometimes shown holding a scroll. She is usually depicted as an idealized Chinese woman, who is young, beautiful, and sexually desirable. In the legends and miracle tales about Mr. Ma's Wife, she uses sexual desire as a skillful teaching device.

A popular female form of the bodhisattva is Kuan Yin of the South Sea. She is depicted in several ways. Sometimes she is shown seated, with one knee raised, on a rock on the edge of the sea, near a grove of bamboo. She has a peaceful demeanor and is encircled by a full moon. She carries a vase containing supple willow branches and has two attendants, a boy and a girl. A white parrot hovers on her upper right side, carrying prayer beads in its beak. Other variations of this figure depict Kuan Yin riding atop the waves of the sea or standing on the back of a large fish partly submerged in the waves. These versions are associated with the sacred island P'u-t'o, a Kuan Yin pilgrimage site.

The various forms of Kuan Yin are often associated with particular locations and with particular legends or stories. This regional specificity reflects the immense size of China and the diversity of its people, among whom Kuan Yin has acquired slightly different qualities and meanings. However, underneath the iconographic variations is the same bodhisattva, who manifests in different forms according to the needs and dispositions of her followers. The forms of Kuan Yin are, therefore, mutually enriching, and she is worshipped with dedicated love in each of her manifestations.

Zen art reflects the calm clarity of mind that is characteristic of Zen meditation, as we read in the following story of a contemporary Zen artist.

Okbong Sunim

Okbong Sunim is an elderly Korean Zen nun and a painter. For the last few years, she has lived in a small flat in Seoul because her arthritis prevents her from following the daily schedule in a nunnery. However, she still wakes up naturally at 3 A.M. each morning and meditates, as she did when she lived in the nunnery.

As she explains, painting is an important aspect of her spiritual practice: "Painting is meditation for me. As soon as I pick up the brush, there is no difference from meditation. However many distracted thoughts might want to arise, there is no place for them when I paint. My mind is empty of distractions, and there is only the painting being painted. It is meditation because there is only one thought."

In addition to her own painting, Okbong Sunim also teaches people how to paint, if she is asked to

Okbong's main artistic work is the traditional Zen practice of painting the Four Gracious Plants: orchid, bamboo, plum blossom, and chrysanthemum. She describes the individual meaning and significance of each plant in loving detail. The orchid is a beautiful representation of nature, highly fragrant; it displays itself without caring for approval or disapproval. The bamboo has the most strength and character and is always the same, straight and green. It is also used for making flutes, as it gives the best sound. The plum blossom is special because it appears in early spring on the bare branches before there are any leaves. Even if there is snow, the plum blossom will come; it has great constancy. The chrysanthemum is the last flower of the year, coming into bloom after all the other flowers have died back; it can survive even the first winter frosts.

Collectively, the Four Gracious Plants are symbolic of beauty, constancy, and integrity. They are challenging to draw, Okbong explains, and doing so requires great strength. Each leaf, however tiny or insignificant, must seem to come alive. Unless each leaf is alive, not dead, she says, the picture is a failure. Bringing the living quality of the Four Gracious Plants into a picture is difficult, but it is worth doing. "An artist must paint pictures, and I cannot not do it," she told me. "When I am ill, I take up the *hwadu* [Korean form of koan]. When I am a little better, I feel I must paint. Then I forget everything else, distracted thoughts and all. So the painting and I become one. Even if I intend to do something else, I cannot; I forget everything, and everything rests naturally."

do so. She teaches her students the importance of meditating and calming the mind before starting to paint, explaining that a turbulent mind makes painting impossible. At the beginning, Okbong says, her students are quick and eager to learn, but they often lack the motivation and endurance to persevere in facing both the technical difficulties of learning to paint well and the task of keeping the mind focused on the painting. The modern world provides many distractions and there are many different things to do, but, with strong motivation and a calm awareness, it is possible to keep going and become a good painter. For her, Buddhism and painting are a natural pairing: "Buddhism is about what appears naturally, about awakening to our nature, and a painting is an expression of ourselves, of our temperament. Each artist displays, just as it is, his or her own character. When we produce a work out of quietness, we show the quiet, a place where there is neither I nor you."

Tibetan Buddhist Art

The rich assembly of Tibetan Buddhist symbols are purely an encapsulation of the manifold qualities of the enlightened Buddha-mind, manifesting as the absolute realization of wisdom and compassion.

—ROBERT BEER, *THE ENCYCLOPEDIA OF TIBETAN SYMBOLS AND MOTIFS*

As we have seen, in Theravada art, the Buddha is sometimes represented by empty spaces such as his footprints, and in Zen art, Buddha-nature is captured in depictions of nature. However, with the rise of Mahayana Buddhism in India, various bodhisattvas and indigenous Indian deities were incorporated into the Buddhist pantheon, providing new iconographic subject matter for Buddhist art. Then, around the eighth century, a vibrant new form of Buddhism developed, known as Vajrayana, or Tantric Buddhism. Vajrayana represents the final flowering of Indian Buddhist culture. It was practiced in India until the twelfth century, when it was annihilated by the invading Muslim armies. During Vajrayana Buddhism's four centuries in India, many of the complex meditative practices centering on visualizations of male and female deities were revealed by the enlightened yogis and teachers known as the eighty-four Mahasiddhas. Carried by traveling translators and teachers, these practices made their way into Tibet, where they continued to flourish after the demise of Indian Buddhism.

As we can see by looking at the suggestive empty spaces of early Buddhist art, then at the ethereal Chinese and Japanese Buddhist paintings of the natural world, and finally, at the extraordinary specific symbolism of Tibetan Buddhist deity figures, there is a noticeable progression in Buddhist art from formlessness to form. It seems that as Buddhism spread and developed, its art forms became more directly representational. However, it is important to remember that, at an absolute level, form and formlessness are not different. This philosophical paradox is famously described in one of the central texts of Buddhism, the Heart Sutra: "Form is empty; emptiness is form. Emptiness is not other than form; form is also not other than emptiness." Thus the various ways of representing Buddha-nature in art are not limited by either form or formlessness. Each symbolic empty space, depiction of nature, or specific deity expresses the ineffable Buddha-nature in ways appropriate for a particular culture and tradition.

The tantras of Vajrayana Buddhism themselves are highly esoteric doctrines. Essentially, Tantric practices require the meditator to visualize a central deity and his or her retinue of attendant deities within a sacred space, known as a *mandala*. Most of these deities are extremely complex, having many arms, legs, and heads in specific color schemes. Details can vary according to the specific version practiced within one of the four main schools of Tibetan Buddhism. Although all of the main deities

Yamantaka, also known as Vajra Bhairava, represents the wrathful aspect of wisdom.

This Tibetan Buddhist deity has nine heads, thirty-four arms, and sixteen legs.

are of Indian Buddhist origin, the Tibetans integrated them into a complete system, making possible a complete path to enlightenment.

Symbolically, these complex deity forms represent the various qualities of Buddhas or other enlightened beings, each color, hand implement, and physical attribute having a precise meaning. Many of the deities depicted in Tibetan thangkas are male, though some are shown in symbolic union with a female consort. Many also show male and female supporting deities surrounding the main figure. Among the most important female deities depicted as the central figure in such paintings are Tara, who was discussed in Chapter 3, and Vajrayogini, considered overleaf.

Vajrayogini

The queen of all dakinis in the Tibetan Buddhist pantheon is Vajrayogini (Dorje Naljorma), the preeminent tantric form of the female buddha."
—JUDITH SIMMER-BROWN,
DAKINI'S WARM BREATH

The Tantric practice of Vajrayogini and her visualized form were originally transmitted by the great Indian Mahasiddha Naropa in the tenth century. Naropa kept the practice secret and taught it only to two brothers in Nepal before it eventually entered Tibet. In essence, the wild, red, seductive form of Vajrayogini symbolizes the transmutation of passionate desire into blissful wisdom. The following description of Vajrayogini is based on one of her main forms known as Naropa's Dakini, or *Nada Khecari* in Sanskrit.

The source or ground upon which Vajrayogini stands is represented as a six-pointed star. In the center of this star is an eight-petalled lotus of various colors, symbolizing her purity. In the center of the lotus is a golden sun disc, which symbolizes her enlightened qualities. She stands like an archer, leaning toward the left, with her right leg extended and her left leg bent at the knee. Her right foot tramples upon the breast of the red goddess Kalaratri, symbolizing the destruction of desire, and her left foot tramples upon the head of the black god Bhairava, symbolizing the destruction of jealousy.

Vajrayogini has one face, three eyes, and two arms. She is ruby red, naked, and extremely lusty. Her right hand holds a curved knife sealed with a vajra held in a downward direction, symbolizing that she severs all of the faults of samsara. Her left hand holds aloft a skull cup full of blood with the nature of nectar, which she pours into her open mouth. Resting upon her left shoulder is a highly symbolic, white, eight-sided staff, called a *khat-*

vanga. This staff is equal to her own height and represents that she is inseparable from her male consort Heruka. She wears five ornaments of human bone, a crown of five skulls, and a necklace of fifty dry skulls. Her body radiates light, and she is encircled by a blazing mass of wisdom fire.

Vajarayogini is a semi-wrathful, powerful, female presence in Tibetan Buddhist art. She is both the consort of Heruka and an individual deity, whose Tantric practice leads to full enlightenment. Originally this practice used sexual imagery and rituals designed to harness the power of these energies in a skillful way, rather than simply suppressing them. Even though this element of the practice is now usually interpreted metaphorically, the power of the symbols remains effective in the transformation of desire.

Many contemporary Vajrayana Buddhist practitioners in the West have Vajrayogini as their yidam, or personal meditation deity. During an elaborate initiation ceremony conducted by a qualified teacher, a prerequisite to all Tantric practice, the practitioner makes the commitment to perform a daily ritual based on Vajrayogini. The instructions for this practice are contained in a sadhana or sacred text and involve reciting prayers, meditating, and visualizing oneself as the deity. This practice is particularly transformational for women, for as Judith Simmer-Brown tells us, Vajrayogini is considered to be the queen of the dakinis. The dakini is a complex symbol in Tibetan Buddhism, with many levels of meaning. *Dakini* is often translated as "Sky Dancer." These figures have the nature of desireless blissful wisdom and are the

most powerful symbol of the feminine in Buddhism. We look at the dakini and what she symbolizes in greater depth in Chapter 6.

In the interview below, a Tibetan Buddhist artist describes her process in a way that reminds us of the spontaneity and creative energy symbolized by the dakini.

Yahne le Toumelin

Yahne is a French artist whose pictures are imbued with color, light, and surreal shifting shapes and objects. She describes her paintings as having an apparitional quality that could be called abstract, visionary, or fantastic. Yahne has also been a Tibetan Buddhist nun since 1968. She is a serious practitioner who has spent many years in retreat. When she went to Darjeeling to be with her teacher, Dudjom Rinpoche, she didn't paint for seven years, starting again only after he encouraged her. In the following interview, Yahne speaks eloquently about the relationship between her art and her Buddhist practices:

Q: *What does being a Buddhist artist mean to you?*
A: What a wonderful thing it is to communicate in our time when the quality of violence and the expansion of hatred seem to slow down the expression of love. I receive a lot of friendly communications from people who've seen my paintings, and whose lives have been helped either by looking at the paintings or by finding the impetus to paint themselves. The art market has discouraged many artists, so I rejoice if my experience may inspire some confidence in people of the

possibilities that everyone has within themselves. This kingdom, this treasure.

Q: *Could you describe your painting process?*
A: [I paint] by the overflowing of energies. Since I have been painting over the last seventy years, I only paint from joy and not to go to sleep in my prayers. The pure turpentine stops me getting colds. Inspiration is part of my breath and is reinforced by the fact that children in the monasteries will eventually benefit from the sale of the art. Nevertheless, I need to be attentive not to try to make my work "beautiful" or "good," because this intention almost always provokes failure, even though the recuperation or dissolution of the failures are often surprising successes. So [painting] is the mystery of the grace that blows where she wants, when she wants.

The most simple part of the process is to select certain forms or colors at random, like a game of dice or chance, and to stay calm in front of that chance, which promotes joy at a given moment. "Given" says I; it's like that! What is bizarre is the reaction of the public in front of what I don't even understand myself! It is frequently passing on the received grace.

Q: *Your paintings are very spiritual but not iconographic. Are you inspired by traditional Tibetan painting?*
A: Of course! My niece who wanted to become a painter like her auntie worked for four years at Sechen Monastery in Nepal to become a traditional Tibetan painter. Her paintings are perfect, and I admire them. The iconography of Tibetan art is the teaching of the visualization which constitutes our practices. They inhabit me! The result that comes out of my hand in my paintings appears to be like somersaults of joy, certainly due to the deities which animate my energies, but very imperfect. An apple tree gives apples, a cow eats grass and gives milk, a painter inhabited by the deities but who doesn't know how to paint according to the Tibetan tradition and only follows her technique gives "that." Curious!

Q: *Has becoming a Tibetan Buddhist nun influenced your work as an artist?*
A: The fact of being a nun is as much a factor of discipline, as much as withdrawal—nun-active or non-active, nun-existence or non-existence. Ordination is a very powerfully transmitted benediction, a deepening of the refuge in the Three Jewels, a clarification of the ideal of desire in this world. The painting of truth is like the word of truth; it depends on the sincerity and faithfulness of the vow—it is the essence of the vow.

Q: *What link do you see between meditation and creativity?*
A: Creativity is the source of life, of the world, and of a transcendence that is itself merely relative truth. Only meditation allows us to go back to the source and to its over-abundant flow, letting the dust that obscures clarity settle. Samsara, the illusory world, can only melt into nirvana, the original state, by the stability of meditation that abolishes duality into the emerging absolute truth.

One of Yahne le Toumelin's paintings, entitled "Trois Joyeux," showing the energies and joy she describes.

Q: *You speak of "non-action," which allows creativity to bloom. Could you elaborate?*

A: To be a nun is the feminine ideal of nun-action, as I've said already. The only obstacle to creativity is ignorance, from where it springs forth. To hang on to the veil that obscures its profusion would paralyze creativity. Blocked creativity, paralyzed in its spontaneity, reinforces the cement-like solidity of the ego, the karmic tendency or mechanism. This ego is reduced to the suffering scream of the anxiety that torments it, and to aggression toward itself and others.

Non-action is opening. Hildegard of Bingen, to mention a European, said: "I have better things to do than to do something," referring to the state of meditation (*shamatha*). Everybody emanates. In a fairy tale, there was a young girl who vomited snakes and scorpions every time she spoke, but when her sister opened her mouth, she produced diamonds. The important thing is to privilege the inner smile by contemplation, the silence of personal action, therefore giving place to that which is waiting within all of us: the nature of awakening! Adamantine nature is all immanent. It is not us who pulls on a blade of grass to make it grow, nor on the tip of a flower to make it bloom! We breathe without acting! And life is given, given, given at each moment, so let's not impose ourselves on life's processes. It's tiring. Rest!

Q: *Could you speak of the experience of being a Tibetan Buddhist nun as a European woman?*

A: Having received an education in European culture and having become a nun, by dropping the concepts maybe I am still a woman, a European, a bourgeois, an artist, covered with labels and references ... by others, but really "I" don't care. I have forgotten for a long time now this wardrobe of concepts, since by practicing Tibetan Buddhism, I have the extraordinary fortune—super snob!—to be clothed by the deities which are in the spirit of the practice of sadhanas and prayers. Wonderful anthropometric profile, isn't it! I have the great luck to be living in a forest hermitage close to my masters; this says it all. So, therefore, I profit from my condition of being a nun and an old European woman.

I so wish happiness to the innumerable beings and to you.

CHAPTER SIX
WISDOM AND COMPASSION

*By thinking and meditating on the factors
of wisdom, and maintaining a sustained
practice of wisdom and altruism with
concerted effort over a long period of time,
you will see a real change in your mind.*

—HIS HOLINESS THE FOURTEENTH DALAI LAMA

The Union of Bliss and Emptiness

The deities in union with their consorts represent a number of things. ...
They represent the union of wisdom and compassion, of bliss and emptiness
and so on. But the idea is always that we are taking two qualities of mind
which become united into one. This is shown in a very graphic way through
the unity of the male and female.

—VEN. TENZIN PALMO, *REFLECTIONS ON A MOUNTAIN LAKE*

Perhaps the most potent symbols of the union of *wisdom*—the discriminating awareness that realizes emptiness—and *compassion*—the skillful means and method of relating to self and others—are the Tibetan Tantric images of male and female deities in passionate sexual embrace. Known as *yab-yum* (or, very occasionally, *yum-yab*, if the main deity is female and the consort male) the central male deity, the *yab*, embraces his consort, the *yum*, who faces him, looking up and to the side. In addition to the qualities mentioned by Ven. Tenzin Palmo in the quotation above, we can also interpret these two deities in sexual union as the archetypes of being, associated with wisdom, and doing, associated with method. Together, they symbolically unite all opposites into the one, called the *Dharmakaya*—the ultimate reality that is beyond all duality in its perfection.

The fact that the yab-yum deities are symbolic of the union of feminine wisdom and masculine compassion has sometimes been overlooked. Doing so has led to mistaken views, such as that Vajrayana or Tantric Buddhism is degenerate and therefore not true Buddhism. Other people have become fascinated with the idea of finding enlightenment through Tantric sexual practices and have mistaken the symbolism for a literal depiction of sexual behavior by Tantric practitioners. Although such practices exist, they are (or should be) undertaken only by the very few highly realized Tantric yogis at the culmination of many years of diligent practice. Mostly, these practices are enacted metaphorically in visualization as part of the ritual of a *sadhana*, or sacred Tantric text. As Ven. Tenzin Palmo says: "The sexual symbolism [in Tantric sadhanas] doesn't mean they have wild orgies in Tantric monasteries."

If we regard the deities as manifestations of feminine and masculine enlightened qualities rather than as male and female figures, we can better understand the principles underlying the symbolism. Although many Tantric deities are depicted with consorts, two Buddhas and their consorts in particular are representations of the union of wisdom and compassion. These are Samantabhadra with his female counterpart and consort Samantabhadri, and Vajradhara, who is depicted either with red Vajravarahi or blue Vajradhatvishvari, depending on which of the four main schools of Tibetan Buddhism is the source of the painting. All three consorts ultimately represent Prajnaparamita, the perfection of wisdom.

Samantabhadra, whose name means "the ever-perfect father," is depicted in sexual union with Samantabhadri, whose name means "the all-good mother." They are both naked and wear no ornaments, symbolizing the pure emptiness of the *Dharmakaya*—the ground of being or fully enlightened mind, which is the union of pure appearance and emptiness. Samantabhadra sits with his hands in his lap in meditative equipoise. His dark blue color represents the formless space of wisdom and shows that his nature is as infinite as the sky, symbolic of the luminosity or apparitional aspect of the Dharmakaya. Samantabhadri is white, and she symbolizes awareness and wisdom. Her nature is limitless space, the state of ultimate truth or emptiness, the apparitionless nature of no form.

In this painting Samantabhadra is shown in union with his consort Samantabhadri. Together these deities represent the primordial union of compassion and wisdom.

Vajradhara, whose name means "the holder of the vajra" wears the jewel and silk ornaments of a fully enlightened being. His consort, Vajravarahi, whose name means "adamantine sow," is naked except for her bone ornaments. Shakyamuni Buddha is said to have manifested in the form of Vajradhara in order to reveal esoteric teachings on the various Tantras. Vajradhara is also an expression of the Dharmakaya; though he arises spontaneously from the luminous radiance of pure light in *Sambhogakaya* form—the visionary or enjoyment body of a Buddha. His feminine consort

Vajravarahi has her arms about Vajradhara's neck, and her face is turned up so that she gazes toward his face. The pair radiates a divine passion that is free from the obscurations of lust and attachment. Vajradhara holds his arms crossed, embracing his consort and holding a vajra (*dorje*, in Tibetan) and bell (*ghanta*, in Tibetan). As we see overleaf, these ritual Tantric implements also symbolize the essence and energy of the masculine and feminine aspects of Buddhism.

The Vajra and Bell

*The vajra and bell are the two main ritual implements that symbolize the
perfections of method or skillful means (vajra) and wisdom or emptiness (ghanta).
When paired the vajra is held in the right hand, and the bell in the left,
representing the inseparable union of method and wisdom.*

—ROBERT BEER, *THE ENCYCLOPEDIA OF TIBETAN SYMBOLS AND MOTIFS*

Vajra is a Sanskrit word meaning "the hard or mighty one"; the equivalent Tibetan word *dorje* means "the lord of stones." Thus the vajra is imbued with the qualities of indestructibility and brilliant hardness, like the diamond, a stone that cannot be cut or broken, except by itself. Essentially, the vajra symbolizes the indestructible state of enlightenment. It is held in the right hand during Tantric rituals. There are several forms of the vajra; the most common in the Vajrayana tradition are the five-pointed and nine-pointed vajras. Many peaceful and wrathful Tibetan Buddhist deities are depicted holding the vajra in their right hands, including deities in union with a consort. When the deity is peaceful, such as Vajrasattva, whose name means "vajra being" or "vajra hero," the vajra represents the adamantine or indestructible scepter of rulership. When the deity is wrathful, such as Vajrapani, whose name means "vajra holder," the vajra often represents an indestructible weapon that can be hurled like a thunderbolt across the heavens.

The feminine complement of the masculine vajra is the bell, best described as a hand bell. Held in the practitioner's left hand in a variety of *mudras* or symbolic hand gestures, it is rung in particular ways at specific points during Tantric rituals. When the bell is rung, the sound of emptiness arises from the void as vibrations, radiates in all directions, and then fades slowly and imperceptibly back into the void of silence from which it came. The symbolism connected to the shape of the bell is extremely detailed and complex. The handle of the bell is actually half a vajra. Thus the bell is said to be "sealed with a vajra," as are many Tantric implements. The mouth of the bell symbolizes emptiness, and its tongue or clapper symbolizes form.

Together the vajra and bell symbolize the perfect union of method—the skillful means of compassionate action to relieve suffering—and wisdom—the discriminating awareness that realizes emptiness. The union of these two complementary qualities is integral to the Buddhist path. Deeper and more complex levels of interpretation become meaningful only when a person starts to practice Tantra under the guidance of a guru. For instance, the vajra symbolizes the practitioner's yidam or personal deity, the central focus of the Tantric practice, and the bell symbolizes the deity's mandala, the sacred palace in which the deity resides. Both are visualized as part of the ritual of the sadhana.

The vajra and bell are also obvious sexual images and serve as symbols of male and female united beyond the dualities of gender. The hollow void of the bell represents the emptiness of the vagina, often described metaphorically as a lotus, while the scepter-like shape and prongs of the vajra represent the penis. Rather than literal sexual union, the use of these implements in Tantric ritual symbolizes the coincidence of emptiness and great bliss. Tantric rituals utilize the natural energy of sexual desire in the practitioner to effect a transformation of consciousness. The practitioner uses the breath to direct these energies into subtle channels in the body. These channels are so subtle they leave no physiological trace and are visualized by the practitioner. Bringing the energy into these channels causes great bliss to arise, while the meditator simultaneously meditates on emptiness, leading to an experience of nonduality.

At another level, the masculine vajra and feminine bell also symbolize the two truths in Buddhist philosophy, conventional truth and ultimate truth. From the conventional point of view—the way we ordinary, unenlightened humans see the world and ourselves—the feminine emptiness or wisdom represented by the bell is paired with the masculine method of compassion represented by the vajra. However, from the ultimate point of view—which is how Buddhas see—these symbols are merely the illusory play of emptiness and form. Thus the union of deities and consorts and the ritual use of vajra and bell both represent that the penetrating insight of wisdom and the skillful means of compassion are inseparable on the path to enlightenment. In order to become skillful in means or method, a Tantric practitioner must cultivate an understanding of *shunyata*—the emptiness of inherent existence of all phenomena. The Tibetan texts state clearly that the spontaneous manifestation of genuine compassion for others is the sign of truly understanding emptiness. This realization is the culmination of the union of wisdom and compassion.

Gampopa, a great meditator who lived in Tibet at the turn of the twelfth century, sums up the importance of this combination: "When we walk, our eyes and feet must cooperate if we are to reach the city of our choice. In the same way, the eyes of *prajna* [wisdom] and the feet of *upaya* [skillful means] must work together when we want to go to the citadel of highest enlightenment." (Quoted in Judith Simmer-Brown, *Dakini's Warm Breath*) As this chapter focuses mainly on the feminine or wisdom aspect, we look next at the feminine deity Prajnaparamita, called the Mother of all the Buddhas and understood to be the ultimate expression of the feminine principle of wisdom.

Prajnaparamita

The worship of Prajnaparamita was very popular among the Buddhists,
and Arya Asanga is credited to have composed one of the Sadhanas
for her worship which is said to confer wisdom and erudition on her devotees.
—BENOYTOSH BHATTACHARYYA, *THE INDIAN BUDDHIST ICONOGRAPHY*

The deity Prajnaparamita is the perfection of wisdom, the Mother of all the Buddhas. The two parts of her name translate as "wisdom" (*prajna*) and "perfection" (*paramita*). From the beginning, in the earliest Indian Buddhist sutras, wisdom was consistently regarded as female. However, at this early stage Prajnaparamita was not depicted iconographically, and the name referred only to the sutras and teachings on the perfection of wisdom. One of these teachings covers the Six Perfections, the activities of a bodhisattva. Of these, the first five—generosity, ethics, patience, joyful effort, and meditative concentration—are considered "masculine" and therefore concerned with method and skillful means. The sixth perfection—wisdom—is "feminine" and therefore concerned with the discriminating awareness that realizes the perfection of wisdom. Authentic cultivation of the first five perfections depends on this quality, as wisdom is the underlying principle of the other perfections.

The name *Prajnaparamita*, however, generally refers to a series of the most important Mahayana Buddhist sutras, known collectively as the Prajnaparamita Sutras. Among these, the most famous is the brief text known as the Heart Sutra, or the Heart of Wisdom, which presents in condensed form the Buddha's teachings on wisdom

Prajnaparamita, the female deity who is the perfection of wisdom and the mother of all Buddhas.

or emptiness. The Heart of Wisdom is presented as a dialogue, a conversation between the great bodhisattva Avalokiteshvara and one of Buddha's main disciples, Shariputra, both, we are told, inspired in what they say by the power of the Buddha's concentration. Because *shunyata* (emptiness)—the lack of inherent existence of all phenomena—is impossible to describe completely in words and can be realized only in meditation, the sutra is characterized by the use of negatives. These list all the things that emptiness is *not*, rather than making the futile attempt of describing what emptiness actually *is*. Thus we are told that in emptiness there is "no eye, no ear, no nose, no tongue, no body, no mind, no form, no sound, no odor, no taste, no object of touch, no phenomena." Abiding in this vast openness, the mind of the meditator is "without obstruction" and therefore experiences "no fear."

In the most famous extract from the sutra, which we looked at briefly in Chapter 5, Shariputra asks Avalokiteshvara how one should train in the perfection of wisdom. Avalokiteshvara replies: "Form is empty, emptiness is form. Emptiness is not other than form; form is also not other than emptiness." These cryptic sentences are as close to a definition of the wisdom that understands emptiness as it is possible to come using language. At first, the sentences seem impossibly paradoxical and seem to contradict themselves. However, through meditation on the central message—that form and emptiness are not different from one another—insights into the nature of emptiness gradually arise in the mind of the meditator. Such insights might include the reflection that all objects, which is what is meant by "form," are impermanent. However long things last, from the few days of a butterfly's life to the centuries it takes for a river to wash away a rock, eventually everything returns to emptiness, "no form."

Such an insight might lead the meditator to examine the nature of objects and to inquire into why they are impermanent. When the constituent parts of objects are scrutinized, the meditator sees that the seemingly substantial nature of all things is an illusion. Everything depends on causes and conditions, such as a chair depending on the tree that provided the wood and the carpenter who made it. Without these and many other interdependent causes and conditions, the chair would not exist. The chair's existence is dependent on the combination of infinitesimal interlinked causes and conditions, and the same is true of every phenomena and being.

Moreover, the chair's existence also depends on our perception of it. We know we sit on chairs; that's what they are for. But is it still a chair if we place a cup of coffee on it? Is it not then, perhaps, a table, as its function has now become that of a table? If a leg is broken off, is it still a chair? If not, then what is it? When we examine objects from this perspective, our view of them as substantial entities with a solid and unchanging existence crumbles. Eventually we arrive at the view that all phenomena, including ourselves, exist in ethereal and dreamlike ways, as a dynamic dance between form and emptiness.

Toward the end of the sutra, the mantra of the perfection of wisdom is proclaimed by Avalokiteshvara: TAYATHA OM GATE GATE PARAGATE PARASAMGATE BODHI SOHA. The mantra can be translated: "Gone, gone beyond, gone absolutely beyond, enlightenment." At a deeper level, the mantra is a reference to the five major steps on the path leading to enlightenment in the Mahayana tradition and their sequential practice until enlightenment is achieved. At each step, a person on the path moves "beyond" (GATE) the previous level of wisdom until enlightenment (BODHI) is finally attained.

Several hundred years after this sutra was written down, the iconographical forms of the great goddess Prajnaparamita arose and came to personify these teachings as the female embodiment of the perfection of wisdom.

Appearance and Symbolism of the Mother of the Buddhas

As the goddess of the Perfection of Wisdom, the iconographic form of Prajnaparamita
probably dates from the early period following the advent of Mahayana Buddhism,
and she is certainly one of the earliest goddesses to enter the Vajrayana pantheon. ...
As the Mother of the Buddhas or Conquerors, she is often identified as the consort
of the primordial or Adi Buddha...

—ROBERT BEER, *PEACEFUL DEITIES OF VAJRAYANA BUDDHISM*

Prajnaparamita is the archetypal female deity because she represents the perfection of wisdom, the feminine quality of discriminating awareness. As she is the embodiment of this quality, she is inseparable from it. However, all female deities and consorts are also referred to by the term *prajna*, wisdom, and so also embody the quality of discriminating awareness. But because *Prajnaparamita* is herself inseparable from the principle of wisdom, all female deities are sometimes called Prajnaparamita, which means they are manifesting or embodying her essence. The name, then, refers both to the quality of wisdom and to Prajnaparamita herself, because their nature is inseparable. Thus when Tara or Vajrayogini, for example, are sometimes called Prajnaparamita, it doesn't mean that they have assumed the form of the goddess Prajnaparamita; it simply means they embody her essence.

The two most important of the nine main forms of Prajnaparamita are Yellow Prajnaparamita and White Prajnaparamita. However, as images of Yellow Prajnaparamita are most frequently found on the painted and carved wooden book covers of the early wisdom texts, we can assume that this is

A detail of Yellow Prajna-paramita from a mural at Tholing Monastery in western Tibet.

the predominant form. She is golden yellow, with one face, two eyes, and four arms. She is exceedingly beautiful, youthful as a sixteen-year-old, and adorned with the silk clothing and jeweled ornaments of a fully enlightened being. Her first right hand is held before her heart in the mudra of explaining the dharma, and her first left hand rests palm upward in her lap in the mudra of meditation of emptiness. The second pair of arms are extended to the level of her shoulders, with the right hand holding a Prajnaparamita text, and the left, a *mala*, a rosary of prayer beads. Some forms of the deity have slight variations of the mudras and ritual objects.

Although she has form, ultimately Prajnaparamita refers to the formless feminine principle; she appears as a deity in order for this principle to be venerated. This principle in the Tantras is sometimes referred to as *Yum Chenmo*, the Great Mother or the Mother of all the Buddhas. Prajnaparamita is called the Mother of the Buddhas for two reasons: First, she is a "mother" because the emptiness of her womb gives rise to form. Second, she "gives birth" to the Buddhas because she represents both emptiness and the penetrating insight that allows the meditator to realize emptiness. The seed of becoming a Buddha is awakening to the nondual wisdom of emptiness that has "gone beyond" all concepts. This understanding allows the meditator to see the true nature of reality: that all phenomena arise from emptiness and pass away into it, and that all phenomena are impermanent and exist only in dependence on causes and conditions. Because she embodies these enlightened

qualities, Prajnaparamita is the Mother of all the Buddhas, past, present, and future. Her nondual nature is summed up:

The meaning of the Prajnaparamita
Is not to be looked for elsewhere:
It exists within yourself.
Neither real nor endowed with characteristics,
The nature [of the mind] is the great clear light.

—QUOTED IN JUDITH SIMMER-BROWN,
DAKINI'S WARM BREATH

This poem reveals that the discriminating awareness that realizes emptiness is potentially present in our own minds. The external Prajnaparamita, whether she is encountered in the sutras, in the feminine principle, or in the figure of the goddess, exists to help us realize this meaning for ourselves.

As the embodiment of the feminine principle in Buddhism, Prajnaparamita—together with Vajrayogini—is closely connected with the dakini, often considered the quintessential female figure in Vajrayana Buddhism. We now turn to the dakini, described overleaf.

The Dakini

The encounter with the dakini is the encounter with the spiritual treasury
of Buddhism, the experience of the ultimate nature of mind in its dynamic
expression as a constantly moving, sky-dancing woman.

—JUDITH SIMMER-BROWN, *DAKINI'S WARM BREATH*

The dakini can be a female meditator, or *yogini*, who has achieved great realizations and the consequent magical powers, or *siddhis*. As well as being embodied in human form, the dakini can also be a manifestation of the enlightened mind of a Tantric deity, existing as a dynamic flow of energy. She can also be a goddess or deity, peaceful or wrathful, such as Vajrayogini, who is often referred to as the Queen of the Dakinis. Much information about the dakini is hidden in esoteric knowledge passed down through the oral tradition by teachers when they perceive their students are ready to work with the dakini energies in their Tantric practice. Thus she is an obscure, complex, and sometimes ambiguous symbol, not easily pinned down or neatly categorized. However, as the dakini is, perhaps, the most important manifestation of the feminine in Buddhism, it is important to investigate who she is.

The Tibetan word for "dakini" is *khandro*, which literally means "space voyager," though this phrase doesn't mean she is an alien from another planet! In this context, "space" is metaphorically referring to emptiness, and "voyager" means someone who has immersed herself in the experience of emptiness. However, the dakini is most commonly called a "sky dancer," and this name powerfully evokes her nature of playful dynamic energy

moving through the vast expanse of emptiness. One of her major iconographical forms depicts the dakini flying through the spacious sky, free, wild, and with her long dark hair flowing behind her. In this form, the dakini is an especially inspiring symbol of liberation for women.

In pre-Buddhist Tibet, dakinis were one of several varieties of demonesses roaming the vast, untamed expanses of this mountainous country. The great mahasiddhas and teachers, like Padmasambhava who brought Buddhism to Tibet in the eighth century, encountered these female spirits and eventually subdued them, making them loyally accept Buddhism into their land. The dakinis were likewise encountered and tamed, but they embraced the Buddhist teachings, learning about, practicing, and protecting them, especially Tantra. This esoteric aspect of Buddhism, with its yogic practices designed to cut through illusion and lead the practitioner to enlightenment in one lifetime, suited the wild, unconventional nature of the dakinis and provided a suitable channel to transform their powerful energies into enlightened action.

Dakinis can be classified into worldly dakinis and wisdom dakinis, though the difference between the two types is not always clear, and they can interchange function and appearance. Early Tibetan texts emphasized the importance of being able to discriminate between the two. Confusing a worldly dakini for a wisdom dakini could be dangerous because a worldly dakini could sometimes embody negative forces opposed to spirituality and act like a demoness, devouring the person she encountered. In her most powerful manifestations, however, a worldly dakini could also embody realizations of the Buddhist teachings. Conversely, assuming a wisdom dakini was a worldly dakini could mean that a precious opportunity for receiving teachings had been lost. In general, the wisdom dakini is more relevant to Buddhist practice, as she is a fully enlightened being capable of bringing others to the awakened state.

This ambiguity in the nature of the dakini is best explained by looking at their early history in India. The first dakinis were minor deities who served more powerful deities like Kali and Durga, the great wrathful Indian goddesses. They were often classified as witches or were thought to be the spirits of women who had died in childbirth. They were much feared, because if angered, it was thought they could call down pestilence and disease. They were also encountered during battles, greedily sucking blood from the recently slain. Similar to the worldly dakinis of the Tibetan tradition, these female spirits lived in charnel grounds, surrounded by the bodies of decaying or half-cremated corpses, wearing clothes made from bits of shroud or flayed human skin and adorned with bone ornaments fashioned from the skeletons of corpses. They were blood drinkers and flesh eaters, feasting on the bodies of the dead. Such horrific behavior belonged firmly outside the mainstream Brahminical

tradition; thus the dakinis were considered to be outcasts who embodied dark, negative forces.

Dakinis were generally connected with blood. They drank the blood of fresh corpses and other unfortunate victims and were associated with the blood of menstruation and female blood rituals. Women of this time were not only considered inferior to men in many ways, but also impure during menstruation and full of insatiable lust. There was fear about women's natural power over life and death, and much social behavior was designed to bring the control of reproduction into the hands of men. Such an unequal society creates a powerful shadow in the collective unconscious, and this shadow would have strengthened and reinforced the dark power of the dakini.

With the rise of the Tantras in India and the veneration of the feminine principle in union with the male, the dakini was elevated from a witch spirit or minor deity into an all-powerful goddess. In Hinduism, the powerful, dynamic female principle is called *sakti*, without which the male energy is impotent. In this way, the dakini became part of the Great Goddess tradition in India.

However, when Buddhist Tantra developed, the power of the feminine principle was interpreted differently, and the feminine started to represent wisdom or emptiness. Nonetheless, the dakini did not lose her witch spirit qualities altogether, because these became subsumed into the worldly dakini. The wisdom dakini became both a protector of the Buddhist teachings and the enlightened female teacher in Buddhist Tantra, though as mentioned earlier, these two aspects of the dakini can overlap.

Encountering the Dakini

Being a dynamic principle, the dakini is energy itself; a positive contact
with her brings about a sense of freshness and magic. She becomes a guide
and a consort who activates intuitive understanding and profound awareness,
but this energy can suddenly turn and pull the rug out from under you
if you become too attached and fixated.

—TSULTRIM ALLIONE, *WOMEN OF WISDOM*

The highly regarded contemporary Tibetan teacher His Holiness Dilgo Khyentse Rinpoche (1910–1991) once told a group of his students about his experience in a significant dream. In this dream, as dusk fell, Rinpoche was circumambulating a *stupa*, or reliquary building, a Buddhist devotional practice to generate merit or positive karma. He noticed an old beggar woman nearby. As he continued his circumambulations, he began to feel concerned for the old woman, as after dusk, she might fall prey to robbers. He approached her to ask if she needed assistance. The old woman lifted her head and, with a dazzling smile, told him that though he had been supplicating her these many years in his meditation practice, he had failed to recognize her. At once, Rinpoche saw her as his personal meditation deity, or *yidam*.

Stories in which the dakini is at first not recognized are common. She often appears in unfamiliar form, in the guise of a beggar woman, or even as a dog. Through the shock of suddenly recognizing her, the conventional mind of the person who encounters her is startled out of its mundane thoughts and conceptualizations, and the dakini points to the clear empty nature of the person's mind. This method is similar to the sudden shock that Zen teachers can give their students by an unexpected slap or other surprising and bizarre behavior. The ability to surprise us into awareness is one of the dakini's main characteristics; she shocks us out of our usual mode of thinking to reveal to us the innate luminous clarity and wisdom of our own mind.

The dakini can appear in dreams, as we see from the story above, but she may also appear as a person, or sometimes only her voice is heard. If we are fortunate and encounter one of her manifestations, we can be sure that it is designed to jolt us out of our complacency and wake us up to our potential enlightened state, currently hidden under layers of confusion. Because the dakini is trying to show us something that is hidden in our mind, she sometimes speaks in an incomprehensible language. The language of the dakinis works through the power of the sounds of the syllables, much the same way as mantras do. The sounds bypass the conventional mind because there is no intellectual component or logical meaning for us to grasp.

Dakinis often appear at twilight or dawn, crossover points between two states of consciousness, when the possibility of opening to our true nature is strongest. In some lineages, the language of Tantra is called the "twilight language," an oral tradition similar to the language of the dakinis. Twilight language and dakini language are comprehensible only in the twilight world, which exists beyond both rational consciousness and the murky depths of the unconscious. At such in-between times, the mind is open to the realm of the dakinis, helping the practitioner reach a state of nondual awareness. In the Dzogchen tradition of Buddhism, one of the practices is called the Song of the Vajra, which is written in the sacred syllables of the language of the dakinis. When it is sung ritually, the sounds vibrate with the enlightened energies of the universe. Practitioners immerse themselves fully in the sound, existing temporarily far beyond the level of personal ego. This immersion leads them toward an experience of nonduality, wherein all experience becomes as one.

The secret language of the dakinis also reminds us that the true meaning of Tantric texts can be revealed only through an initiation from a qualified teacher who forms part of an unbroken lineage to the source of the teaching. Such restrictions keep the teachings pure, hiding them from those who are uninitiated and therefore not ready to hear them. These days

Manibhadra, one of the great Indian Mahasiddhas, flying blissfully through the sky like a dakini.

Tantric texts are easily available in books for anyone to read, but the meaning beyond the words can only be realized through an initiation ceremony and subsequent practice under the guidance of a guru.

Machik Lapdron

Machik Lapdron, the great yogini who founded the Cho[d] lineage in Tibet,
meditated on retreat in a sanctified cave during the spring of her forty-first year.
In the middle of the night, the majestic savior Tara appeared to her surrounded by a host of dakinis and gave detailed empower-ments and blessings.

—JUDITH SIMMER-BROWN, *DAKINI'S WARM BREATH*

One of the most remarkable examples of a woman yogini who was a manifestation of the dakini is Machik Lapdron. She lived in eleventh-century Tibet (1055–1152), a great period for Buddhism, with much dialogue between Indian and Tibetan scholars and yogis before Buddhism was wiped out in India. Though she was a real woman, Machik Lapdron's biography includes many legendary details. We are told that Machik was a bright and remarkable child, who was born with three eyes, giving no pain to her mother and surrounded by auspicious signs that she would be a highly realized being. At an early age, she became a professional reader. Such people, who read quickly and clearly, traveled to the homes of devout lay Buddhists, most of whom could not read them-selves, and recited texts for their benefit and for the accumulation of merit. One of the texts Machik read in this way was the Prajnaparamita Sutra.

Machik Lapdron depicted in the pose of a dancing dakini, holding a hand drum (*damaru*) and a bell.

Machik first studied Buddhism with Geshe Aton, who then sent her to the highly realized teacher Lama Dra. He saw her potential to become a great teacher herself and taught her the meaning of the Prajnaparamita texts she had been reciting. She quickly attained a high realization and dedicated herself to meditation in her teacher's monastery. After some time, another teacher, Sonam Drapa, came to see Machik and listened to her explanation of the Prajnaparamita. He saw she still had subtle levels of attachment preventing her reaching full enlightenment and advised her how to let go of these final hindrances. Shortly afterward, her behavior changed, and she left the monastery, wearing rags and seeking the company of beggars and outcasts, a sign of true renunciation.

She continued seeking teachings from great masters. On several occasions dakinis appeared in dreams and manifestations and told her to engage in Tantric sexual practices with the yogi Topabhadra as her consort. She was told that these activities would cause the Buddhist teachings to spread and create a new lineage. She went to Topabhadra, and the two traveled together in central Tibet, combining Buddhist practice with having a family, two sons and a daughter. When Machik was thirty-five, she received prophecies from the dakinis to return to Sonam Lama for further empowerments into other Buddhist practices. He recognized her as a great dakini and gave her the name Dorjeying Phyugma, meaning "woman rich in indestructible space." She then spent time practicing with the Indian yogi Phadampa Sangye, who became her main teacher

because, through his inspiration, she developed the practice of Chod. She continued receiving and giving teachings until, at the age of forty, she had become famous throughout Tibet.

When she was forty-one, she meditated in a cave and received teachings and blessings from Tara, as described in the quotation above from Tsultrim Allione. Shortly afterward her husband visited with their children, who then became their mother's disciples. Many other people came to hear her teach and took her as their guru. She taught her disciples many Buddhist meditations and Tantric practices, especially the practice of Chod. Near the end of her life, she participated in a great debate with some learned Indian teachers. They had come to challenge her, as they doubted her abilities, but by the end of the encounter, they had nothing but profound respect for this amazing yogini. When she was ninety-eight years old, Machik left this life and went to the Land of the Dakinis.

The Chod practice founded by Machik Lapdron in Tibet is a lineage of Tantric meditation based on the Prajnaparamita teachings. Chod is practiced to cut through self-cherishing, attachment, and the other mental afflictions that prevent us from awakening to our true nature. Using the discriminating awareness that arises from meditation, practitioners develop insight into the nature of themselves. They discover they have no solid inherent existence but are the sum of constituent parts, such as mind, body parts, and consciousness, arising in dependence on causes and conditions. From this understanding of the emptiness of the self arises spontaneous compassion for other beings.

Khroma Nagmo, the black wrathful form of Vajravarahi, surrounded
by her retinue of dakinis. She
herself is a dakini, and her
practice is employed in the
Chod ritual.

balanced over a fire. The visualization continues with the practitioner mentally chopping up his or her body and ritually placing the bits in the skull cup, which becomes huge. As the fire "cooks" the bodily substances, they are transformed into nectar, which is offered to all beings to drink their fill. Throughout the ritual, the practitioner is mindful that everything is of the nature of emptiness, the ritual, the practitioner, and all other beings. The ritual is completed with further contemplation on the empty nature of reality and with prayers for the eventual enlightenment of all beings.

We can see the link between this practice and the behavior of the worldly dakinis in the charnel grounds, though Chod is a practice that transforms all negativities using the imaginative power, not the actuality, of charnel ground rites. The practice also has similarities with alchemy. The alchemist's intention is to transform base material into something divine, and the fire used as a means to alchemical transformation is also a metaphor for purifying the inner spirit. Although we might find the visualized rituals of the Chod startling, they are simply the Tantric expression of cutting away delusions, such as clinging to the ego, that prevent us from awakening to the enlightened state. Tantra utilizes everything in life as the path to transforming our

Chod means "to cut." After preliminary practices, including tranquil abiding meditation to calm the mind, the practitioner visualizes that his or her consciousness exits the body through the top of the head. The consciousness then transforms into a wrathful dakini who cuts off the top of the practitioner's head, creating a skull cup, which is placed on a tripod of three human heads

consciousness, even our own bodies, and the Chod ritual is a powerful way to cut our attachment to body and ego.

Balancing the Ultimate and the Conventional

The celebration of women's experience and the feminine principle in Buddhism that has been the subject of this book is only half of the whole. As we have seen, the female aspect is inseparable from the male, and it is the nondual union of feminine wisdom and masculine compassion that we seek in our Buddhist practice. This union of opposites is the perspective of ultimate truth. However, we must also take into account the view from conventional truth, which acknowledges that there are differences between women's and men's opportunities and experiences on the Buddhist path. The history of Buddhism tells us clearly that women did experience prejudice from the male spiritual hierarchy and that this discrimination explains to some extent the imbalance between the numbers of great male and female gurus, teachers, artists, deities, and yoginis. However, a woman attending a modern Western Buddhist center today is unlikely to experience discrimination based on her gender. As a vibrant, living spiritual tradition, Buddhism evolves as it encounters new cultures.

Taking a last look at Tara, we see how she embraces both the ultimate and conventional views in her enlightened behavior. As we recall, Tara vowed to take only female rebirths until all beings are liberated, as a skillful way of working to overcome discrimination against women. But she also acknowledged clearly that the ultimate purpose of encountering the Buddha's teachings is to practice them without the distraction of gender differences, as revealed in her statement: "Here no man, no woman." Tara's approach epitomizes the Middle Way path advocated by the Buddha, which acknowledges all, but avoids extreme views. Working creatively with this balance between ultimate and conventional views in our own lives is the most appropriate way for us to approach the Buddha's teachings.

This nun and monk standing together symbolize the balanced view that ultimately, on the Buddhist path to enlightenment, gender is irrelevant.

Bibliography

Allione, Tsultrim. *Women of Wisdom*. London: Arkana, 1986.

Batchelor, Martine. *Walking on Lotus Flowers*. London: Thorsons, 1996.

Batchelor, Stephen. *The Awakening of the West*. London: HarperCollins*Publishers*, 1994.

Batchelor, Stephen. *Buddhism Without Beliefs*. New York: Riverhead Books, 1997.

Batchelor, Stephen. *The Tibet Guide*. Somerville, Mass: Wisdom Publications, 1998.

Bhattacharyya, Benoytosh. *The Indian Buddhist Iconography*. Calcutta: Firma K L Mukhopadhyay, 1958.

Beer, Robert. *The Encyclopaedia of Tibetan Symbols and Motifs*. London: Serindia Publications, 1999.

Beer, Robert. *Peaceful Deities in Vajrayana Buddhism*. (Not yet published.)

Beer, Robert. *Wrathful Deities in Vajrayana Buddhism*. (Not yet published.)

Blofeld, John. *In Search of the Goddess of Compassion*. London: George Allen & Unwin, 1977.

Chung, Tsai Chih, ed. *The Book of Zen*. Singapore: Asiapac Books, 1990.

Coleman, Graham, ed. *A Handbook of Tibetan Culture*. London: Rider, 1993.

Das, Surya. *The Snow Lion's Turquoise Mane*. New York: HarperCollins*Publishers*, 1992.

Dowman, Keith. *Masters of Enchantment*. Rochester, Vermont: Inner Traditions, 1988.

Dowman Keith. *Sky Dancer*. London: Routledge & Kegan Paul, 1984.

Grilli, Elise & Nakamura, Tanio. *Sesshu*. Rutland & Tokyo: Charles E. Tuttle Co., 1960.

Gyatso, Kelsang. *Heart of Wisdom*. London: Tharpa Publications, 1986.

Gyatso, Tenzin (the Dalai Lama). *The World of Tibetan Buddhism*. Boston: Wisdom Publications, 1995.

Kyi, Aung San Suu. *Freedom from Fear*. London: Penguin, 1995.

Landaw, John & Weber, Andy. *Images of Enlightenment*. Ithaca, N.Y.: Snow Lion Publications, 1993.

Murcott, Susan. *The First Buddhist Women*. Berkeley, Calif: Parallax Press, 1991.

Palmo, Ani Tenzin. *Reflections on a Mountain Lake*. Ithaca, N.Y.: Snow Lion Publications, 2002.

Rabten, Geshe. *Echoes of Voidness*. Somerville, Mass: Wisdom Publications, 1983.

Reps, Paul (compiled by). *Zen Flesh, Zen Bones*. London: Pelican, 1971.

Rinpoche, Bokar. *Tara the Feminine Divine*. San Francisco, Calif: Clearpoint Press, 1999.

Shaw, Miranda. *Passionate Enlightenment*. New Jersey: Princeton University Press, 1994:

Simmer-Brown, Judith. *Dakini's Warm Breath*. Boston: Shambhala Publications, 2001.

Snelling, John. *The Buddhist Handbook*. London: Rider, 1998.

Willson, Martin. *In Praise of Tara*. Somerville, Mass: Wisdom Publications, 1986.

Willson, Martin & Brauen, Martin. *Deities of Tibetan Buddhism*. Somerville, Mass: Wisdom Publications, 2000.

Yu, Chun-fang. *Kuan-yin*. New York: Columbia University Press, 2001.

Acknowledgments

I would like to thank Liz Puttick and Debbie Thorpe for bringing this book to fruition. Brenda Rosen's skillful editing was invaluable, as was Lynda Marshall's sympathetic picture research. Thanks to Marc Baudin for translating Yahne's interview. I am deeply grateful to each of the contributors for their stories and reflections about what it means to be a Buddhist woman. Special thanks to my dear friend Martine Batchelor, who generously shared her considerable knowledge and understanding, and who pointed me in the right direction. And lastly I thank my partner Robert Beer for his wise insights into the symbolism of Buddhist deities and for his love and support throughout the writing of this book.

Index